# STATE ORGANS
Transplant Abuse in China

# STATE ORGANS
Transplant Abuse in China

Edited by David Matas and Dr. Torsten Trey

Seraphim
EDITIONS

Library and Archives Canada Cataloguing in Publication


State organs : transplant abuse in China / edited by
David Matas and Torsten Trey.


Includes bibliographical references.

ISBN 978-1-927079-11-9


1. Transplantation of organs, tissues, etc.--Government
policy--China. 2. Transplantation of organs, tissues, etc.--Corrupt
practices--China. 3. Transplantation of organs, tissues, etc.--Moral
and ethical aspects--China. 4. Prisoners--Abuse of--China. I. Matas,
David II. Trey, Torsten, 1967-

RD120.63.C55S73 2012      362.1979'500951      C2012-903994-2

In-House Editor: Kathryn McKeen
Cover Design and Typography: Rolf Busch

Dedication: "The Lives and Opinions of Eminent Philosophers by Diogenes
Laertius", translated by C. D. Yonge *Life of Solon*, Section X.

Published in 2012 by
**Seraphim Editions**
54 Bay Street
Woodstock, ON
Canada N4S 3K9

Third Printing, 2013

*Printed and bound in Canada*

*When will we end injustice? When those who are not victims*
*feel as much outrage as those who are.*


Solon

# CONTENTS

9   Introduction      *David Matas and Torsten Trey*

16   Transplant Medicine at      *Torsten Trey*
a Crossroads

27   Polluted Sources      *Arthur L. Caplan*

35   The Spoils of Forced Organ      *Ghazali Ahmad*
Harvesting in the Far East

49   How Many Harvested?      *Ethan Gutmann*

68   Organ Transplantation      *Erping Zhang*
Issues in China

77   Numbers      *David Matas*

94   Persecution of Falun Gong      *David Kilgour and Jan Harvey*

108   The Impact of the Use of Organs      *Jacob Lavee*
From Executed Prisoners

114   How Should the Academic      *Gabriel Danovitch*
Community Respond?

119   Responsibilities of International      *Arne Schwarz*
Pharmaceutical Companies

136   The Mission of Medicine      *Maria A. Fiatarone Singh*

143   Contributors

# Introduction

The purpose of medicine is to provide care for those who suffer. The Hippocratic Oath commits medical doctors not to do harm. Yet, in China, we can see that this ethical principle is violated by the taking of organs from prisoners, including prisoners of conscience. These prisoners of conscience are mostly practitioners of Falun Gong, but also include Uighurs, Tibetans and others.

While organ transplant abuse exists in many countries, China presents a unique situation, a country where state institutions are heavily implicated in the abuse. How do we stop the killing in China of innocents for their organs?

There appear to be three basic answers to that question. One is to end the persecution against the particular group from which organs are sourced such as Falun Gong, which was banned in China in 1999 because the then leader of the Communist Party, Jiang Zemin, feared that its popularity would threaten the ideological supremacy of the Party. The second is to end the network of slave labour camps in China, euphemistically called "re-education through labour camps", where detained Falun Gong are mostly housed and which have become vast forced organ donor banks. The third is to end the killing of prisoners for their organs in general. End the killing of all prisoners for their organs, and then the killing of prisoners of conscience for their organs would inevitably cease.

Human rights advocacy is an effort in mobilization. It is easy enough to say that human rights belong to all humanity. However, getting people to do something about it is not so easy. Yet, as Greek lawmaker Solon noted over two thousand five hundred years ago, we shall succeed in ending injustice and abuse when those who are not the victims are as outraged about the injustice and harm as those who are the victims.[1]

Parliamentarians, media, ethicists, international human rights organizations, international lawyers, government foreign affairs officials, human rights educators and intergovernmental human rights officials all ought to be allies in the effort to combat organ transplant abuse in China. By experience, the group above all that took up the challenge and moved in greatest numbers and most cohesively to do something to end that abuse was the medical profession.

In some ways this was understandable, since it was their profession which was being abused. As well, they had forms of influence, through peer pressure, that others did not have. In addition, their knowledge of the science of transplantation and the people involved meant that many of them knew that this abuse could be and was happening.

After the first version of the report *Bloody Harvest* came out in July 2006, David Kilgour and David Matas travelled around the world to combat the abuse their report identified. Conferences of transplant professionals turned out to be fruitful venues. Co-editor David Matas participated in the Congress of The Transplantation Society in Sydney, Australia in 2008 and in Vancouver in 2010, the American Transplant Congress in Philadelphia in 2011 and Congress of the European Society for Organ Transplantation in Glasgow in 2011. He met many concerned, knowledgeable professionals including several of the contributors to this book.

The unethical organ procurement practices in China led to the foundation of the NGO "Doctors Against Forced Organ Harvesting" (DAFOH). Executive Director of DAFOH and co-editor, Dr. Torsten Trey, made contacts with many doctors from around the world who shared the same wish to end this unethical practice.

This book builds on these contacts and this developing coalition of medical concern. It is a statement of the problem, a report on the efforts made to date and a call for continuing efforts to combat the abuse.

———————————————

The first essay, by Dr. Torsten Trey, introduces the topic of the book. His presentation shows how transplant medicine in China got to the point where it is now. His essay analyses organ sources and shows that the officially acknowledged source of organs, prisoners sentenced to death, cannot be the only explanation for organ sourcing.

The second essay, by Dr. Arthur Caplan, focuses on the ethical complications which arise from using prisoner organs for transplantation with the claim that there is free consent. The author reminds us of the responsibilities of the medical profession and lays out options doctors have.

Dr. Ghazali Ahmad, the author of the third essay, shares his experience about the shifts in transplant tourism in his country, Malaysia, in recent years and how transplant treatments in China for Malaysian patients changed after 2006. The essay is a reminder that following ethical requirements is a pre-condition for best practices in medicine.

Ethan Gutmann, the author of the fourth essay, provides a survey based estimate of Falun Gong murdered for organ transplants. The author relies on a range of detailed interviews of individual witnesses.

The author of the fifth essay, Erping Zhang, addresses the history of transplant medicine and laws in China. He attempts to explain the particular vulnerability of the Falun Gong movement to being targeted for organ harvesting.

In the sixth essay, David Matas looks at the same issue as Ethan Gutmann, the issue of numbers, using a different methodology. Though the techniques are different, the conclusions largely coincide.

The seventh essay, by David Kilgour and Jan Harvey, provides perspective on Falun Gong as well as a historical timeline of events surrounding unethical organ harvesting in China. References to specific individual victims of organ harvesting add further reality to the story of victimization.

The author of the eighth essay, Dr. Jacob Lavee, recounts his personal path after a patient of his in Israel received a heart transplant on short notice in China. He developed ideas later used for a new transplant law in Israel, a law which generated a more than sixty percent increase in organ donations in one year.

In the ninth essay, Dr. Gabriel Danovitch elaborates on the responsibility of scientists to pursue ethical research. The author urges the application of ethical standards when publishing research results in medical journals.

The tenth essay, the work of Arne Schwarz, addresses the use of transplant related drugs tested in clinical trials in China and elaborates on the question of how pharmaceutical companies react to the fact that over ninety percent of transplant organs in China stem from prisoners. The author advocates that data unethically acquired in clinical trials should not be used for scientific findings.

In the eleventh and last essay, Dr. Maria A. Fiatarone Singh writes a personal essay about her involvement in promoting ethics in transplant medicine. Despite her not being professionally part of the transplant field, the author felt compelled to take an active role in calling for an end to unethical organ harvesting in China.

⸻

The book comes out at a time of leadership transition in China. Organ transplant abuse is part of the mix.

David Kilgour and David Matas began their investigative work in this area because a woman using the pseudonym Annie, then in Washington, D.C., told the *Epoch Times* a story of how her ex-husband harvested corneas of Falun Gong practitioners in Sujiatun Hospital between 2003 and 2005. *Epoch Times* published the story in its March 17, 2006, edition. Annie said other doctors at the same hospital harvested other organs of these victims, that Falun Gong were killed during the harvesting and that their bodies were cremated.

Annie's interview led to a controversy about whether or not she was telling the truth. The Government of China, as one might expect, denied what she said. The Coalition to Investigate the Persecution of the Falun Gong (CIPFG), a Washington, D.C. based NGO, then asked David Kilgour and David Matas to investigate her claims.

Sujiatun is a district in the city of Shenyang. Shenyang is a city in the province Liao Ning.

Bo Xilai, considered to be a "princeling" because his father was Vice Premier of China, was appointed Mayor of Dalian City in Liao Ning Province from 1993 to 2001. He was further appointed Deputy Secretary of the Chinese Communist Party for Liao Ning Province in 2000. From February 2001 to February 2004, he was Governor of Liao Ning Province.

While he was in Liao Ning, Bo developed a reputation as a brutal leader in the persecution of Falun Gong. The period that Annie's husband worked in Sujiatun Hospital and the period that Bo Xilai was Governor of the province in which the hospital was located overlapped.

Bo, in February 2004, went to Beijing where he became Minister of Commerce. While Minister of Commerce, Bo Xilai travelled around the world to promote international trade with China and investment into China. His travelling gave victims the opportunity to serve him with lawsuits for his role in the persecution of Falun Gong in Liao Ning Province. Lawsuits commenced against him in thirteen different countries including Canada, the U.S., and Australia.

Bo's vulnerability to foreign lawsuits became a reason to move him out of his then position and prevent him from acquiring any new position which required foreign travel. Bo went from Minister of Commerce in Beijing to Mayor of Chongqing in November 2007 and became then a member of the 25 member Communist Party Central Committee.

Wang Lijun was the head of the Jinzhou City Public Security Bureau On Site Psychological Research Center (OSPRC), Liao Ning Province from 2003 to 2008. He conducted research on a lingering injection execution method which would allow organ removal for transplants before the person died from the injection. He conducted further research to prevent patients who received organs of injected prisoners from suffering adverse effects from the injection drugs.

In September 2006, he received the Guanghua Science and Technology Foundation Innovation Special Contribution Award for his research and testing of this lethal injection method. In his acceptance speech, he talked about "thousands" of on-site organ transplant cases from injected prisoners in which he and his staff participated.

Wang worked under Bo in Liao Ning Province in 2003 and 2004. In 2008, shortly after Bo was moved from Beijing to Chongqing, Bo brought Wang from Liao Ning Province. Wang held various positions in public security in Chongqing and in 2011 became deputy mayor of the city under Bo.

Wang, to international amazement, in February 2012 attempted to defect to the United States, seeking asylum in the U.S. Consulate in Chengdu. Neither the Americans nor Wang have made public the reason for this attempted defection, though there are many rumours. The Americans decided against giving Wang asylum, and he was handed over to the Chinese authorities. He remains in detention as this introduction is being written.

Bo was expected to become a member of the nine member Communist Party Standing Committee in the fall of 2012. Instead, shortly after Wang's attempt at defection, Bo was purged from his position in Chongqing and from the Central Committee.

Chinese Prime Minister Wen Jiabao, at a closed Communist party meeting in Zhongnanhai shortly after these events, is reported to have addressed organ harvesting and Bo Xilai's involvement. A source attributes to Wen these remarks:

> Without anaesthetic, the live harvesting of human organs and selling them for money – is this something that a human could do? Things like this have happened for many years. We are about to retire, but it is still not resolved. Now that the Wang Lijun incident is known by the entire world, use this to punish Bo Xilai. Resolving the Falun Gong issue should be a natural choice.

What happens in China behind closed doors at Communist party meetings is, by its very nature, not a matter of verifiable public record. What could be seen though by anyone at this time was the lifting of censorship on the killing of Falun Gong for their organs. In late March 2012, search results about organ transplants on the officially sanctioned Chinese search engine Baidu showed information about the work David Kilgour and David Matas did, *Bloody Harvest* and the involvement of Wang Lijun in organ harvesting.[2]

It is hard to let a genie just a little way out of the bottle. Knowledge spreads, even in a society subject to censorship. Selective leaks and references to organ transplant abuse by those involved in the power struggle within China are bound to have an effect beyond the power struggle itself, to have a real impact on the abuse. Our hope through this book is to magnify that impact.

David Matas
Dr. Torsten Trey

---

1 "The Lives and Opinions of Eminent Philosophers by Diogenes Laertius," translated by C. D. Yonge *Life of Solon*, Section 10.

2 Cheng Jing "Wen Jiabao Pushes for Redressing Falun Gong, Source Says," *Epoch Times* April 9, 2012.

# Transplant Medicine at a Crossroads

## Unethical Organ Procurement Practices in China Lead Medicine *Ad Absurdum*

### TORSTEN TREY, MD

## Turning Point

In the beginning of 2006 a tiny news report unnoticed by mainstream media caught my attention: transplant doctors in China were allegedly harvesting organs from prisoners of conscience without consent and while alive. I was puzzled. Shortly thereafter, I read the initial version of *Bloody Harvest*,[1] an investigative report about the aforementioned allegations co-authored by David Matas and David Kilgour. The first report delivered 17 pieces of evidence, including phone recordings in which doctors from Chinese hospitals stated that they had "fresh organs from Falun Dafa practitioners". The report suggests that organs were deliberately harvested from adherents of the persecuted spiritual practice.

That July, I attended the World Transplant Congress in Boston, where I sought conversation with doctors from China. One of them, Dr. W. Liu, was a senior liver transplant surgeon from Tianjin Oriental Transplant Center, one of three hospitals in Tianjin that perform transplantations. When asked how many liver transplantations his hospital performed, he replied, "two thousand liver transplants last year". I was surprised that so many liver transplants were performed at only one hospital and questioned where the organs came from, but did not get a satisfying answer. Later I talked to another Chinese doctor who, at that time, was working in a transplant-related research lab at the University of Hanover in Germany. In our conversation he mentioned he had received invitations from two hospitals in China to build a new transplant department in their hospitals. I asked why the transplant field was growing so fast in China despite not having a public organ donation program, and where the organs came from. The doctor replied, "Ask the Falun Dafa practitioners outside," referring to the practitioners who posted information about the live organ harvesting outside the convention center. The answer was his way of saying that the organs came from adherents of this persecuted spiritual practice.

After looking further into organ procurement practices in China, I learned about the systematic organ harvesting from executed prisoners and realized the extent to which ethical standards were being violated. It reminded me of the human experiments conducted in Nazi concentration camps. And because medical doctors were involved in this crime against humanity, I felt the responsibility to respond to this malpractice from within the medical profession. The year 2006 became a turning point in my medical career as I decided to lead the work of "Doctors Against Forced Organ Harvesting" (DAFOH).[2]

## The Subject

Transplant medicine is a relatively young medical specialty that has successfully contributed to saving or prolonging people's lives and to improving quality of life. Aside from new transplant materials, transplant medicine depends largely on human organs, donated by human beings. In this regard, organ procurement is essential to transplant medicine.

The success of transplant medicine is accompanied by a dramatically increased demand for organs. The organ procurement is based on free consent, and operates through public organ donation programs. Due to a limited organ supply and increasing demand, the waiting time for matching organs has increased. Sometimes the waiting time is longer than the life expectancy of the patients. These circumstances have contributed to the development of organ trafficking – people travel to facilitate transplantation. In some cases, the recipients might travel abroad to receive a transplant; in other cases, the donor travels to the country where the recipient lives. In either case, the recipient is, generally speaking, purchasing the transplant organ from the donor.

The decisive criterion in this practice is that the donor stays alive after donating an organ, usually a kidney. This model is even tempting to health insurance companies,[3] as an early transplantation is financially still more cost efficient than health expenses needed to cover the healthcare during the waiting time for a transplant, especially in the case of kidney failure and hemodialysis.

Purchasing organs for transplantation is ethically speaking arguable, a gray zone. However, in China, transplant medicine has crossed the line and gone beyond this gray zone. In contrast to the global phenomenon of organ trafficking where the donor stays alive, organ procurement practices in China are mostly based on the "intended death" of the donor. By saying "intended death," I refer to the death that does not occur by accident or in the course of nature, but rather, through the decision or intention of other people, for example, by the verdict of a judge in a court trial or just by bluntly killing people who have been arbitrarily outlawed by the communist government, as in the case of Falun Dafa practitioners.

In countries with public organ donation programs, organ donation is based on the donor's free consent, with a possible variation of "opt-in" or "opt-out" choice. In contrast to this free donation practice, in China, the decision to "donate" organs is imposed upon certain vulnerable groups and minorities, like death row candidates and prisoners of conscience. In other words – prisoners are "forced" to donate their organs. Usually the official explanation is, "the death row candidate wants to redeem by donating his organs". However, organ harvesting from executed prisoners does not meet the ethical standard of "a freely consented donation". In 2006 the World Medical Association (WMA) Council adopted a "Resolution on organ donation in China"[4] in which it explicitly states, "prisoners and other individuals in custody are not in a position to give consent freely, and therefore their organs must not be used for transplantation". In the same resolution "the WMA reiterates its position that organ donation be achieved through the free and informed consent of the potential donor". Furthermore, the WMA demands that "the Chinese Medical Association (CMA) condemn any practice in violation of these ethical principles and basic human rights and ensure that Chinese doctors are not involved in the removal or transplantation of organs from executed Chinese prisoners" and that "China immediately ceases the practice of using prisoners as organ donors".

In 2007 the CMA promised to the WMA at the General Assembly in Copenhagen to end the practice of using organs from executed prisoners for transplantation, except for direct family members. Five years after Copenhagen, the official statements from China continue to be that 90% of the organs from deceased donors stem from executed prisoners.[5]

I would like to take a closer look at the official explanation that death row candidates "want to donate" their organs. Between 2003 and 2009 there were only 130 free organ donations in all of China.[6] It is commonly acknowledged that there is a traditional reluctance within the Chinese population to donate organs. This goes back to the cultural belief system influenced by Confucius that the body must stay intact after death. If there is a widespread traditional reluctance in the Chinese population to donate organs, to the extent that public organ donation programs do not gain a foothold in China, how can it be explained that this low consent percentage suddenly turns into a seemingly high "consent rate" among death row candidates? It would suggest that either consent has been imposed on the prisoners, or that the ethics guidelines of the WMA are correct and that imprisonment indeed influences the free choice that one would have otherwise in freedom. And, from a different aspect, if the consent rate is not close to 100%, how many prisoners are needed to provide enough organs for 10,000 to 20,000 transplantations every year? Let alone that not every death row candidate is suited to serve as an organ donor.

Regardless of the consent process, organ procurement in China is mostly based on the death of the donor, a death that is induced by man and did not occur by accident or in the course of nature. We are talking about forced organ harvesting from executed prisoners and prisoners of conscience, including cases where the "donor" is still alive when his organs are being harvested.

## A Closer Look into Organ Procurement Practices in China

In China the practice of harvesting organs after execution started in the mid 1980s. Executed prisoners have admittedly been the main source of transplant organs since then. Despite an estimated high but steady number of executions, the transplant figures saw a dramatic increase of transplantations starting after 1999. *The China Daily* newspaper reported a peak of 20,000 transplants in 2005. In parallel, the number of transplant centers in China increased from approximately 150 to 600 between 1999 and 2006. More than the exponential increase of transplantations after 1999 can tell, the significant expansion of the infrastructure of transplant centers expresses an unexpected confidence in an apparently boundless number of organs. This is even more surprising in the absence of an effective public organ donation program at that time. Up to today, efforts to initiate public organ donation programs in China have met with a sluggish response. Hence, it appears as if the confidence in the expansion of transplant centers and transplant medicine was a reflection of the expectation that the killing of people for their organs would continue in the future.

We are facing here a new and unprecedented reality in medicine. Killing people – under the name of "executing prisoners" – has become an essential part of transplant medicine.

Aside from the sudden increase of transplant figures after 1999, another phenomenon has been observed. Websites from Chinese hospitals have offered to provide matching transplant organs to foreign patients within a waiting time of 1 to 4 weeks. In addition, Chinese universities invited foreign transplant specialists to perform demo transplantations with several weeks or months advanced notice, including the question of what time of day they would prefer to operate.

If more than 90% of transplant organs stem from executed prisoners, and therefore, if one mainly depends on the verdicts of the judges to have access to the organ source, how can one schedule a transplantation in such advanced notice? The Chinese law demands that death row candidates have to be executed within 7 days after verdict,[7] thus one would be able to schedule a transplantation within 7 days in advance, but not beyond. Hence, one may wonder how one can schedule a transplantation 14 or more days in advance, including the time of day. One may wonder if the number of executions is even higher than estimated, thus providing a sufficiently large amount of organs, or if the death sentences might be influenced by blood type and tissue factors,[8] or if there is actually another organ source that is not covered even by a figure as high as "90%".

Amnesty International estimated that in China approximately 2,000 prisoners are executed per year; other estimates go as high as

8,000 executions per year. That is roughly 6 to 22 executions per day. The average number of transplants that are needed to reach the annual figure of 10,000 to 20,000 transplants is 27 to 54 transplants per day. I leave the rest of the math to the experts who may take into account that there are factors that would exclude prisoners from being eligible for organ donation, such as age and a specific prevalence of infectious or other diseases among prisoners.[9] In the end, only a limited group of executed prisoners might be eligible for organ donation, and not all of their organs may be suitable for transplantation. Blood type, tissue factors, and the short time window add more variables to the equation, turning the fast and specific response to transplant demands into a bigger question. Given these circumstances, even the official explanation that the organs come mostly from executed prisoners is not satisfying, although one might feel, sad to say, "appeased" by the statement that "90%" of the organs stem from executed prisoners. The death row candidates alone don't provide a sufficient explanation for the mysterious organ sourcing numbers in China. How can this "on-demand" organ procurement system in China be explained? One is inclined to say that, aside from the official explanation of executed prisoners, there must be another group of organ donors, and we assume that these are detained people who are used as a stand-by, living source of organs, ready to be organ harvested at any given time.

In 2006, David Matas and David Kilgour published the first version of their investigative report *Bloody Harvest*, and we learned about significant evidence that practitioners of the spiritual movement Falun Dafa[10] had become the main target for this pool of living organ donors. Subject to persecution and torture since 1999, Falun Dafa practitioners are being illegally held in detention in the hundreds of thousands, marginalized and dehumanized by the Chinese communist party.

I, myself, became alert when I spoke with a Falun Dafa practitioner who, during two years of detention, was blood tested 10 times without having had any health issues. Taking blood samples is costly. Why would detained Falun Dafa practitioners receive specific physical examinations (including x-rays, ultra-sound, blood tests) while at the same time being subjected to brainwashing, labour work, torture or torture death? The medical examinations were certainly not aiming for the health benefit of the victims, as ending the torture and persecution would reach that goal immediately without additional costs. As a matter of fact, many Falun Dafa practitioners who suffered from persecution in detention reported about similar medical examinations, including having received unspecified injections. It makes one think that the medical examinations of Falun Dafa practitioners are performed in order to build up a systematic medical data bank, a systematic categorization of potential living organ donors.

How did it come to this point? We assume that approximately between 1999 and 2001, a short time after the persecution against the Falun Dafa movement had started, the previous practice of harvesting organs from executed prisoners and the persecution against Falun Dafa merged together, turning the otherwise worthless cadaver of a torture death victim into a "profitable biomass," a source of transplant organs. Websites of Chinese hospitals advertised kidney transplants for USD 60,000, and liver transplants for USD 100,000. Some military hospitals even bragged on their websites that organ transplantation was their #1 revenue source. Yet, this still might be difficult to comprehend or to believe in the 21st century – a large number of detained prisoners of conscience has been scanned and turned into a pool of living, though not consenting, organ donors. Once the blood and tissue factors match with a transplant seeker, the matching Falun Dafa practitioner is killed and his organs harvested.

This scenario is so terrifying that one is rather inclined to not believe it. And it is exactly this "too-cruel-to-be-true" pattern that served as best cover for a decade. One might want to recall the reply of Supreme Court Chief Justice Felix Frankfurter to Jan Karski when the latter reported his eye witness accounts of the Holocaust in Nazi-German concentration camps. Frankfurter replied, "I am not saying that you are lying, but I just cannot believe what you told me." As we know, the disbelief did not prevent that people continued to be killed in gas chambers.

Consider this: Under communist China's rule, a Falun Dafa practitioner has no basic rights and his life is worthless. He cannot even expect legal defense when a judge sentences him to labour camp or to death. Tens of thousands of Falun Dafa practitioners have been tortured, and even tortured to death within the past 13 years of persecution. Under these conditions, without any respect left for the human life and without having to fear any legal consequences, it was just a small step to use a living being as a profitable organ source instead of beating him or her to death.

When confronted with this horrifying statement that living people are being killed on demand to harvest their organs, critical minds might ask for hard evidence. Concerning the question of what hard evidence could be, they may ask for video footage, eyewitness reports by the "donors" or doctors. However, the crime of organ harvesting from living people is extremely and exceptionally rare and cruel, and hence, it can be reasonably understood that this practice is rather well covered and hard evidence is difficult to be procured. The donors won't survive the procedure, and the doctors who are involved, including military doctors, would take a high risk to expose themselves. At this stage of investigating the organ harvesting from living people, it is rather irrational to absolutely insist on "hard evidence" or, if not provided, to reject all pieces of evidence altogether. At court trials, it is not uncommon not to have so-called "hard evidence," yet a verdict can still be delivered based on circumstantial evidence. Due to a combination of more than 50 pieces of circumstantial evidence and strict professional analysis as addressed in the latest report by David Matas and David Kilgour, it is reasonable to draw the conclusion that the live organ harvesting did exist and still goes on. As medical doctors, it is not our role to make a judgment, but with the collected information at hand, we should feel responsible to call for international attention and further investigation on this topic. We encourage those who insist on having "hard evidence" to use their energy and call for professional inspections in Chinese hospitals.

Having said that, the International Red Cross inspection of the Theresienstadt Ghetto in 1944 may serve as a warning for us – the inspectors misinterpreted the deadly gas chambers as clean shower facilities, a false conclusion with fatal consequences. With all the circumstantial evidence at hand, and being aware of the Theresienstadt deception, we need to call for professionally performed inspections in China, before this crime against humanity grows further.

Recent announcements from Chinese officials to end the practice of harvesting organs from executed prisoners in the next 3 to 5 years may sound commendable, but they are not. We are not only calling for an immediate halt of harvesting organs from executed prisoners, but also for an immediate halt of harvesting organs from living, detained Falun Dafa practitioners and other prisoners of conscience. But as long as Chinese officials do not mention or admit the organ harvesting from Falun Dafa practitioners, and do not provide permission for professional inspection teams to visit respective hospitals, as long as this crime against humanity is kept secret, the international medical community runs the risk of being deceived like the International Red Cross inspectors in the Theresienstadt Ghetto.

## Reactions

The practice of harvesting organs from executed prisoners in China has caused distinct opposition and reactions from the medical community and other professions. Aside from medical organizations and associations, like DAFOH, TTS and WMA, many individual doctors have started to oppose the unethical organ harvesting practices in China. Some of them have taken the initiative to investigate on their own, for example Prof. Francis Navarro.[11] Pretty much all the medical doctors I have spoken with agree that the medical profession should not take part in doing harm and that the organ harvesting practices in China do not meet the ethical standards and must end.

The work of "Doctors Against Forced Organ Harvesting" (DAFOH) is an exemplary resource for those interested both from the medical and non-medical professions to learn more about the unethical procedures in China. DAFOH has co-hosted or organized forums and participated in panel discussions, including a panel discussion in the U.S. Capitol. The forums had great response and doctors in the audience stepped forward to offer support. Signature lists were reflections of the support that we received – usually about 90% of the attendees signed our petition. Our efforts also contributed to several publications in medical journals, including a letter in JAMA.[12] DAFOH's mission is to raise awareness and to call for an end to the unethical organ harvesting practices. And there are many colleagues who share the same wish. Upon requesting a statement from The Transplantation Society (TTS) in early 2012, President-Elect Dr. Francis Delmonico replied:

> TTS is opposed to the use of organs from executed prisoners, and through the efforts of the Declaration of Istanbul Custodian Group, TTS opposes the presentation of reports from China at international congresses and the publication of papers from China

in the medical literature that involves the use of organs from executed prisoners.

U.N. Special Rapporteur on Torture, Prof. Dr. Manfred Nowak has submitted several reports to the U.N. Human Rights Council, in which he also addressed organ harvesting in China. He stated, "the (Falun Gong) practitioners were given injections to induce heart failure, and therefore were killed in the course of the organ harvesting operations or immediately thereafter".[13] He also indicated that using death row inmates as explanation for the main organ source is "inconclusive". During his visits to China, Dr. Nowak also encountered slow response to his requests and pointed out a lack of transparency.

Today, the medical practices and research studies are interwoven worldwide. Such international networking can go along with cultural or social differences. Yet, independent from these differences, respect for human life remains the common denominator in medicine everywhere without which medicine would lose its honorable purpose. In China, some of the communist rulers have turned their hatred against Falun Dafa into a crime against humanity, using the medical profession as a tool for their hatred. Killing human beings for their organs in order to provide transplantation for others is not only a crime against humanity but also incompatible with the mission of medicine and leads transplant medicine as well as medicine in general *ad absurdum*. Now it is up to the medical profession to react.

---

1 Matas, D. and D. Kilgour. *Bloody Harvest: The killing of Falun Gong for their organs* (Woodstock, Canada: Seraphim Editions, 2009)

2 www.dafoh.org (Last accessed April 24, 2012)

3 Bramstedt, K.A. and Xu J, "Checklist: Passport, Plane Ticket, Organ Transplant," *Am J Transplant.* 7(7)(2007):1698-1701

4 http://www.wma.net/en/30publications/10policies/30council/ cr_5/index.html (Last accessed April 24, 2012)

5 http://www.theepochtimes.com/n2/china-news/chinese-netizens-ask-hard-questions-about-organ-transplantation-202781.html (Last accessed April 24, 2012)

6  Yu X., "Cultural taboos and corruption," *Newschina.* (July 1, 2011):17-19

7  Chinese Code of Criminal Procedure; Article 211

8  Beholz, S. and R. Kipke, "The Death Penalty and Organ Transplantation in China: The Role of Academic Heart Surgeons," *J Heart Lung Transplant* 26 (2007):873–5.

9  http://articles.boston.com/2012-03-24/world/31230487_1_huang-jiefu-organ-donations-harvesting-organs (Last accessed April 24, 2012)

10  http://faluninfo.net/ (Last accessed April 24, 2012)

11  http://www.theepochtimes.com/n2/world/organ-harvesting-in-china-26322.html (Last accessed April 24, 2012)

12  Trey, T., A. Halpern, and M.A. Fiatarone Singh, "Organ Transplantation and Regulation in China," JAMA, Vol 306, No. 17 (November 2, 2011):1863-4

13  http://www.theepochtimes.com/n2/china-news/manfred-nowak-china-organ-harvest-20596.html  (Last accessed April 24, 2012)

# Polluted Sources:
## Trafficking, Selling and the Use of Executed Prisoners to Obtain Organs for Transplantation

ARTHUR L. CAPLAN, PhD

Many have long condemned the forced and coerced use of living persons to obtain organs for transplantation.[1, 2] The international community should find this practice ethically repugnant because it is the ability of the individual to give his or her consent that makes the removal of an organ from a living person at all ethically legitimate.

Why do such practices endure? Why are so many people being trafficked for kidneys all over the world? The answer is the demand for kidneys and the tolerance of exploitation of the poor.

There is a tremendous shortage of kidneys, not only in the U.S. but worldwide. Demand continues to escalate. Why? There are more and more people trained to do transplants. The outcome of transplantation has improved significantly. More people who are living longer need and are becoming eligible for transplantation. And sicker people, those with cancer, mental illnesses and other comorbidities are becoming eligible for transplantation.

When I first became interested in the field of transplantation, the people who were eligible for transplant were between 30 and 50 years old, could have no other illnesses or diseases, had to have family support and had to have some sort of employment.[3] The idea behind the government in the U.S. reimbursing the cost of kidney transplantation was, in part, because these would be people who would go back to work and lead lives that would help them repay the cost of their kidney transplant. Today we are seeing not only solid organs transplanted but also composite tissues – face, limb, voice box and uterus. Some of these transplants have been done in China, others done in Spain, Saudi Arabia, Turkey and other nations. Demand is growing worldwide both for new forms of transplants and older procedures such as kidney and liver transplants.

The field has not only expanded with regard to what can be done in terms of transplants but also who it is that is considered eligible to receive one. The average age of a person who gets transplanted in the USA today is closer to 55 years of age for a kidney; they usually have other comorbidities/medical problems and often do not go back to work. The number of centers doing kidney transplants has expanded from dozens in the 1970s to hundreds today. So it is easy to see why demand has exploded and continues to grow.

Other factors affect the availability of cadaver organs. If you make cars safer, mandate wearing seatbelts and installing airbags and penalize driving drunk, these good public health measures save lives. But they do diminish the number of people that are available for cadaver organ donation.[3]

So, over the decades, there has been improved safety and efficacy, more people in need, more programs and less carnage involving motor vehicles, and that equation leads to increasing pressure on the supply of kidneys and other organs. Many nations have turned to living donors to try and meet the demand for kidneys, and to a much lesser extent livers. The turn toward living sources has taken place in the context of an ethical framework that has achieved international public support over many years. When transplant was in its infancy in the 1960s, there were ideas around about how to get organs that included paying people to sell their organs and simply taking them from the dead without asking.[3] These ideas were rejected. The argument that won the day was that the individual has the right to control what happens to his or her body through altruistic giving even after death, even if selling or taking might benefit or save the lives of others. Partly respect for altruistic giving was out of respect for the individual's cultural, religious, personal and moral values. Partly it was out of respect for the idea that the body itself should not be made the object of commerce.

Mainly the norm of altruistic giving triumphed out of respect for the idea that people should have the dignity of not having to sell body parts as a way to make a living.

Sale leads to trafficking, exploitation or both. When someone argues[4, 5, 6, 7] that the very poor, prisoners or other vulnerable groups can and should be allowed to choose to sell an organ, I am more than a bit skeptical about the nature of that "choice". A person at the bottom of any society's economic hierarchy has very few options. And choice is not simply a matter of not being coerced. It is also a matter of having options available to pick amongst. If I put you in a desert, naked, with no resources except your hands, legs and a lot of sand, are you free to do what you want? Yes. Is there much you could do? No. You are, thus, not really autonomous. You are not really able to choose because you have no options. And that is what is often overlooked in current debates about letting the very poor or institutionalized sell their body parts. The fewer the choices a person has, the more it is exploitation rather than choice that describes a decision to sell a kidney or a baby or to be a prostitute.

So I am skeptical that the very poor for whom selling organs is most likely to be offered can really choose to sell. Their very circumstances – loaded with debt, children going hungry, collection agencies hounding them, possessions being seized – give them no choice but to sell their bodily parts – for men, kidneys and for women, their sexual organs.[8] Should not a humane society offer some alternative to this exploitation beyond condoning the practice? Add in the inability to regulate or police the selling of organs and you have an inhumane option offered to the most vulnerable by criminals and thugs. This is not choice consistent with voluntarism but exploitation consistent with barbarity.

Choice is also the linchpin of protection against public distrust that organ procurement will lead to the mining of the dying to get parts for others. You must choose, not have others choose for you. You must decide whether you want to be an organ donor, not your doctor or anyone else. If free altruistic choice is not the moral core of how organs are obtained then the public will, rightly, begin to worry that because someone is poor, not famous, not popular, they will not receive aggressive care if they enter a hospital. They will be seen merely as potential parts for someone else richer, more famous or more celebrated.[9] So choice is crucial, both out of respect for the dignity of the individual and the protection it provides against premature organ harvesting.

Which brings us to the current practice of trafficking in kidneys using living persons who some say "choose" to be involved. What we see in trafficking around the world is that the poorest of the poor are exploited. Many of the same people who traffic in children and women for prostitution and slave labour also traffic in organs. It is very difficult to police trafficking internationally. Criminal gangs move quickly and operate in nations where police and government authority are either minimal or easily corrupted.[10]

The sole protection that anyone has against being trafficked against their will is to hold every transplant team accountable for knowing where the organs that they transplant come from and knowing that the organs that they use have been obtained through voluntary, altruistic consent. Knowing the provenance of where the organs come from must be the ultimate responsibility of the transplant team. They have to verify that consent was obtained. They have to verify that the person voluntarily gave that organ up. They cannot say they don't know where the organ came from. They cannot say they don't care where the organ came from. If trafficking is to stop then the transplant community must agree not to use any organ unless it is known how it was obtained and that the source consented to give it. And that, by the way, applies to both the living and the dead. It is the responsibility of the transplant community to make sure that they verify the provenance of all organs.[1]

What about the use of executed prisoners to obtain kidneys and other organs for transplant? China is the nation most reliant on this practice. It is a practice utterly at odds with voluntary, altruistic free choice.

China does not have any cadaver organ system for obtaining organs and tissues for transplant. However, it has huge demand for transplants. Some estimates are that as many as a million people in China could benefit from a transplant. There is also a big business in China in transplant tourism. Chinese hospitals are all over the Internet saying "come here, and we can get you a liver transplant within weeks if you pay a high fee".

Official Chinese government statistics state that they have done more than 20,000 livers in the past 10 years. They also state that

1,475 livers came from living donors. They admit they do not have a cadaver system. Then where do they get their organs? Where they are getting them is from executed prisoners. That is the only possible source.[11]

Consent in China for a prisoner is non-existent. The execution is timed for the convenience of the waiting recipient, particularly if that recipient is a transplant tourist. If you are going to go to China, and you are going to get a liver transplant during the three weeks you are there, then that means someone is going to have to schedule an execution. They will need to find a healthy prisoner with the right blood type and tissue type and the right size liver and have that prisoner ready to harvest before the transplant tourist needs to leave. There is no chance that simply waiting for someone to die randomly or be executed on a fixed schedule will wind up matching a transplant tourist's biology. The prison authorities have to find potential donors, screen them for health, blood and tissue type and kill them while the tourist is in China.[12, 13] That is simply killing for hire on demand. It is beyond credulity to think that consent or altruism play any role in such a system.

To get organs on demand, speed is important since organs are frail once the heart stops circulating blood. Prisoners, having been pre-typed blood and tissue type, are shot in the head and then organs are removed in a special ambulance on the spot. The reason that this can be done is that it is all handled by the military. In China, the military operates many of the prisons and most of the people involved in killing for parts are military doctors. With the military in charge of the prison system, and with the military able to bring to bear the medical expertise to get it done, China can use a source of organs that would not work in other nations that have capital punishment such as parts of the U.S.[13, 14]

Just recently the Chinese Vice Minister of Health said that, in fact, China is using executed prisoners as their primary organ source. He said plans are being formed to establish an organ transplant response system, meaning a cadaver system such as exists in North America, Europe, Singapore, South America and the rest of the world. The minister said organ shortage is the bottleneck in the development of Chinese organ transplantation because they don't have voluntary cadaver donations by citizens; executed prisoners have become the main source of organs in transplant operations in China.[15] The minister stated that the current strategy of relying on executed prisoners would be changed in the next three to five years.[15, 16]

The present system of relying on organs from executed prisoners ought to be changed. But, it should not be changed in the next three to five years. It ought to be changed in the next three to five minutes!

What is the case for China or the world tolerating five more years of executing prisoners on demand? The practice is immoral, violates basic human rights and conflicts with international standards of the transplant community.

In China, prisoners are in prison for a variety of reasons. Some are there for political reasons; sometimes they are there due to their religious or spiritual beliefs, like Falun Gong, and sometimes because they are Tibetans or other groups looking to secede from China.[11, 12] The list of crimes meriting death is long and indefensible. So when some argue for the use of executed prisoners as organ sources,[17] it must be remembered some of those who will die will be political dissidents, spiritual dissidents and people who have committed petty crimes. Executing anyone on demand for their parts is unethical but it is especially so when those being executed are in prison for political views, spiritual beliefs or petty crimes.

One of the great tragedies of our time has been the lack of vocal condemnation by human rights groups, governments, NGOs, journal editors, religious groups, prison advocacy groups and the general biomedical community of this morally abhorrent situation in China. Murdering people for their parts without consent, some of whom don't belong in prison at all, in horrific ways, is one of the worst practices ongoing in all of medicine. Yet articles describing Chinese experience with transplantation continue to appear in medical journals. People from China come and talk about transplantation and what their experience and outcomes are at many conferences and meetings. Research goes on in China involving drugs and other ways to improve transplantation sponsored by international pharmaceutical companies.

China, for many reasons, is a place we want to encourage to enter into and interact with the international community. This may lead to a certain reluctance to condemn killing for parts schemes. It must be a condition of entry, however, that we not sacrifice our own core values such as the immorality of killing to obtain organs in seeking to encourage engagement with China. The world ought to adopt a much stronger stance against this unacceptable source of organs. At a minimum boycotting all papers and talks from China concerning transplantation involving prisoner sources should be standard practice amongst editors and meeting organizers.[18]

Getting organs from those who sell them while alive or who are mined for them after their execution are both immoral. Sale quickly devolves into trafficking and exploitation. Execution on demand is on its face unethical. Neither source ought to have any place in the field of transplantation.

1  Caplan, A.L. and C. Prior. "Trafficking in Organs, Tissues and Cells" and "Trafficking in Human Beings for the Purpose of the Removal of Organs." Joint Council of Europe/United Nations Study, 2009.

2  "The Declaration of Istanbul on Organ Trafficking and Transplant Tourism and Commercialism," *The Lancet* 9632 (2008): 372-3.

3  Caplan, A.L. and D.H. Coehlo. *The Ethics of Organ Transplants* (New York: Prometheus, 1998)

4  Cherry, M.J. *Kidney for Sale by Owner: Human Organs, Transplantation and the Market* (Washington, D.C.: Georgetown University Press, 2005)

5  Cherry, M.J. "Medical Innovation, Collapsing Goods, and the Moral Centrality of the Free-market," *The Journal of Value Inquiry* 40(2-3) (2006): 209-226.

6  Cherry, M.J. "Embracing the Commodification of Human Organs: Transplantation and the Freedom to Sell Body Parts," *Saint Louis University Journal of Health Law & Policy* 2 (2009): 359-377.

7  Satel S. "The Case for Paying Organ Donors," *Wall Street Journal*,2009 http://online.wsj.com/article/SB10001424052748704322004574477 840120222788.html

8  Scheper-Hughes, N. "Rotten Trade, Millenial Capitalism, Human Values and Global Justice in Organs Trafficking," *Journal of Human Rights* 2 (2003): 198-203.

9  DeVita, M., & A. L. Caplan, "Caring for Organs or for Patients? Ethical Concerns about the Uniform Anatomical Gift Act," *Annals of Internal Medicine* 147 (2009): 876–879.

10  Budiani-Saberi, D.A. Delmonico FL, "Organ Trafficking and Transplant Tourism: A Commentary on the Global Realities," *American Journal Transplantation* 8 (2008): 925-8.

11  https://www.dafoh.org/

12  Matas D., and D. Kilgour. *Bloody Harvest: the killing of Falun Gong for their organs* (Seraphim Editions: 2009)

13  Malone A. "China's hi-tech 'death van' where criminals are executed and then their organs are sold on black market," Mail Online web site. http://www.dailymail.co.uk/news/article-1165416/Chinas-hi-tech-death-van-criminals-executed-organs-sold-black-market.html

14  Gutmann E. "The Xinjiang Procedure." *Weekly Standard* (December, 5, 2011) http://www.weeklystandard.com/author/ethan-gutmann

15  China says will end organ harvesting of prison inmates http://english.ntdtv.com/ntdtv_en/news_china/2012-03-23/china-says-will-end-organ-harvesting-of-prison-inmates.html

16  Shi B.Y., and L.P. Chen. "Regulation of organ transplantation in China: difficult exploration and slow advance," *JAMA*. 306, 4 (2011):434-435.

17  Wang M., and X. Wang. "Organ donation by capital prisoners in China," *J Med Philos*. 35, 2 (2010):197-212.

18  Caplan A.L., H.A. Rockman, and L.A. Turka. "Editorial position on publishing articles on human organ transplantation," *J Clin Invest*. 122, 1 (2012): 2-2

# The Spoils of Forced Organ Harvesting in the Far East

GHAZALI AHMAD, MD

The kidney transplant program in Malaysia started in 1975 with a living related donor involving a sibling donor-recipient pair. A year later a deceased donor kidney transplant followed suit. Due to the compromised quality of life associated with long term dialysis treatment and encouraged by the consistently high rate of success of the renal transplant surgery, many patients with end stage renal disease were driven by a combination of despair over lifelong dialysis and high hopes of full restoration of normal health along with the freedom to undergo renal transplantation. With the limited number of donated organs locally and a long waiting list for transplantation, some patients ventured beyond the national border in a desperate attempt to get a kidney transplant. The rule and principle of the ends justifying the means apply in these cases.

The serious imbalance between the perpetually increasing high local demands for and persistently limited supply of donated kidneys had created a fertile ground for unscrupulous individuals working either singly or in a larger organised, albeit clandestine, racket. They capitalised on the misery and desperation of the patients in need of kidney transplants by offering a seemingly efficient and effective shortcut solution to the organ shortage. A stage was set and the ground fertile for the syndicates to capitalise on the supply-demand imbalance and the desperate wish for kidney transplant by patients who could not accept the fate of life-long dialysis.

## Indian Connections

In the late eighties and early nineties, many patients from Malaysia travelled to various parts of India, particularly to the slum stricken city of Chennai (Madras as it was popularly known then) in the southern state of Tamilnadu, where syndicates in organ trafficking would arrange for such patients to receive organs from live unrelated and, in all cases, hard core, poor donors who, on their own, were in desperate need of financial assistance, very often for basic necessities of life. Most of the transplant recipients would never meet their respective kidney donors as the circumstances leading to and the procedures involved in the procurement of the kidneys were shrouded in mystery. One such recipient was able to trace the address of the donor from his hospital contacts. Before his departure home after a "successful" transplant surgery, he made his way to the donor's residence. Much to his shock and anguish, he learned that the young man who had sold one of his kidneys for his transplant surgery had passed away as a result of post-operative complications. His sense of guilt lingered on for a prolonged period after his return home, knowing that the young man had become a victim of a syndicate which fulfilled his transplant need. In most cases, the transplant recipients would return to Malaysia with a medical summary written on formal letterhead describing the surgical procedure, the list of prescribed medications, laboratory results which indicated the best state of the graft function achieved and the clinical progress post-surgery. The referral documents usually bore the signature of the clinician managing the patient, giving the impression that the clinical process and procedures were transparent, professionally performed and devoid of ethical controversies. While many transplant recipients enjoyed satisfactory graft function without remarkable adverse outcomes, some patients developed significant complications including severe infections and acute allograft rejections upon return to the home country which required additional diagnostic and therapeutic procedures from public hospitals. Significant and serious donor-related complications in the transplant recipients included post transplant viral hepatitis and HIV infection. Additionally, many patients experienced financial hardships as they needed to purchase expensive immunosuppressive medications in addition to spending their hard earned life savings to pay the syndicate members for their transplants. All these gradually came to an end when the

Indian government introduced a legislation in 1993 which banned organ transplants involving recipients who were non-citizens. The ban effectively stifled the syndicates' activities for a brief period.

## From Madras to Guanzhou

As it turned out, the closure of the Indian organ trafficking activities gave rise to the opening of a new link with what eventually turned out to be a much larger syndicate in illegal human organ trading in the Asia Pacific region emanating from several cities in The People's Republic of China.

Data from the Malaysian Dialysis and Transplant Registry, published by the Malaysian Society of Nephrology annually since 1993, clearly showed that the source of kidneys obtained in China was provided by syndicated, arranged financial transactions. Members of the trafficking ring would reach out by subtle means to the dialysis patients in the hemodialysis units or those waiting to see their kidney specialists in hospital outpatient clinics in various parts of the country.

In a typical case, a patient on regular in-centre hemodialysis treatment would suddenly be found missing from a scheduled regular treatment. When checked by the centre nurse (usually by a phone call), the patient or relatives of the patient would report that the patient had gone overseas for a short holiday. When the patient reappeared a few weeks later, he or she would present with a face masked appearance and have a medical summary from the transplant centre in China indicating that the patient had undergone a renal transplantation plus a description of the transplant procedure together with the necessary clinical details (see copies of such letters which follow).

**Selected medical summaries of transplants involving kidneys from executed prisoners for foreign patients from "Organ Transplant Centres" in China (Nanning City, Guangzhou City, Fuzhou, Kunming)**

June 6,  2006

To whom it may concern

## Information on Mr ██████████████

Dear Doctor

███████████ male, 58years old ,was hospitalized on March 25, 2006 with the diagnosis of Chronic Renal Failure, Uremic stage.

After hospitalization, he underwent the operation of  the kidney replacement. The serum creatinine dropped steadily after his operation .He recovered better than ever and could go back home. The last diagnosis was as follows:

1.Chronic Renal Failure, Uremic stage

2.Hypertension

3.Type 2 DM on insulin

The immune inhibitor scheme   and   other medicines were as follows:

| | | |
|---|---|---|
| Cyclosporine | 200mg   8Am | 200mg 8Pm |
| Cellcept | 0.5 | Q8h |
| Prednisone | 30mg | Qd |
| Aciclovir | 0.2 | Tid |
| Adalat | 20mg | Q12h |
| Diltiazem | 30mg | Q12h |
| Metoprolol | 12.5mg | Q12h |
| Furosemide | 40mg | Bid |
| Cefuroxime Axeril | 0.25 | Bid |
| Famotidine | 20mg | Bid |
| Heptodin | 0.1 | Qd |
| Novolin R | 8u H Am 14u H Noon 22u H Pm 30min before the meals | |
| Novolin N | 4u H 11pm | |

Current laboratory results were shown below:

2006-6-5      Cyclosporine   blood   levels 286.5ng/ml

2006-6-5   Bun7.4mmol/l, Cr106umol/l,UA392umol/l

2006-6-5 WBC9.48×10⁹  /L      N71%   L18.8%   M9.3%

PLT 243×10⁹  /L     HGB 87g/L

Renal Physician ██████████████

# 广州医学院第二附属医院

## The Organ Transplantation Center of the Second Affiliated Hospital of Guangzhou Medical College

Add: 250 Changgang Dong Road, Guangzhou city, China.　Postcode: 510260
Tel: (020) 34152559 (Office)　Fax: (020) 34152892

## MEDICAL REPORT FOR : █████████

Date of Admission: 2005 – 12-06
Date of Discharge: 2006 – 02-07
Diagnosis on Admission: Chronic Renal Failure due to Hypertension Nephropathy

## INTRODUCTION :

Complete body check of heart, lung, liver, upper digestive tract, kidneys, eyes, ear, nose, throat did not indicate restriction for kidney transplantation surgery.

PRA and HLA data obtained in hospital lab .The donor's HLA was a good match to her's. Good match donor organ was identified on 2006-01-19and transplantation operation was performed the same day under general anesthesia.　Prior to surgery, Zenapax 50mg; iv drip, ATG 100mg iv drip and MMF 1000mg (MMF 500mg Bid after the operation). Very little bleeding during operation, no transfusion was required. 20% Albumum 50ml x 2, and MP500mg were used.

After operation, the patient stayed in the transplantation ward. Catheter was removed on the forth day while the drainage tube in incision was removed on the thirth day. Ureter stent has been eliminated from natural urination on the fifth day. The incision got infection at the tenth day because of the fatty. We cleaned and sutured the wound again. Then she had a good recovery.

## MEDICATION :

Immunosuppressant: FK506+MMF+Pred. Initial Dosage for FK506 was 0.07mg/kg; MP was 500mg for the first day and 250mg was used to the thirth day, ATG was 100mg for the first two days and 50mg for the third till the fifth day. After MP, Prednisone 30mg was used a day, subsequently reduced to 20mg/d after two weeks.

# 福建省第二人民醫院腎移植中心

Renal Transplantation Center. Second People's Hospital of Fujan Province,
No. 13 hudongzhi Road, Fuzhou 350003 P.R.CHNA
Tel: +86 591 87878276          Fax: +86 591 87855604

## TO WHOM IT MAY CONCERN

NAME : ███████████          SEX: male   AGE : 17
HOSPITALIZATION TIME: 2005/12/07   to   2006/01/23
DIAGNOSIS: reflux nephropathy and Uremia
OPERATION AND DATE : cadaveric renal transplantation (2006/01/11)
HISTOCOMPATIBLITY TESTS : Blood type O-O
                          PRA (-)
                          Lymphotoxity test 4%
                          HLA: 3MM

OPERATION METHOD :
  The artery of the graft was anastomosed to extra iliac artery of the recipient by
end-side, and the vena was an end-side anastomosis to extra iliac vena too .The
ureter anastomosed with the right top of bladder through under-muscural tunnel
of bladder. The graft was located to right iliac fossa in extra-peritoneum.

POSTOPERATIVE COURSE:
  The urine output of first postoperative 24 hours is 9700 ml. In the
postoperative 7 days SCr is 102 umol/L.   SCr is 110umol/L in the postoperative
12 day. Then there is no rejection within the postoperative 12 days. He is
discharged in the postoperative 13 day.

IMMUNOSUPPRESSIVE THERAPY:
  Postoperative   0 day: MP 1.0 VD, Simulect 20mg IV
                  1-2 day: MP 0.5 VD
                  4day: Simulect 20mg IV
                  3-10day :prednisone 20mg, Gengraf 125mg BID, MMF 0.75 BID
                  11- day :prednisone 20mg, Gengraf 150mg BID, MMF 0.75 BID
LABORATORY TESTS: HB 11.6g/dl,   WBC 6000,   PLT 302,   ALT 8,
    .(2006/1/20)          TBIL 6.1umol/L, Cr 96 umol/L, BUN   6.0mmol/L,
                          Blood glucose 4.8 mmol/L
CsA   LEVEL : postoperative 7day154.78ng/ml (C0) and 933.81ng/ml(C2)
              postoperative 12day 113.20ng/ml (C0) and 772.04ng/ml(C2)
MEDICINE: Gengraf 150mg BID, MMF 0.75 BID
          Prednisone 20mg QD, Norvase 5mg QD
Professor ████████
2006/1/23 ████████

南华大学附属第二医院

Date: July 23, 2006.
To whom it may concern,
Consultant Nephrologist,
Hospital, Malaysia.

## Dear Doctor:

**Re:** ███████████

**Passport No:** ███████

Mr. ████ had consulted me recently for a review. He is on anti-rejection treatment and following up at your hospita

According to the results he present to me, it shows: ①the new kidney function is stabilization, Scr:89μmol/l.② the blood glucose is in the reference range.③the cyclosporin level($C_0$ 19/07/2006) was 232ng/ml.

He had been advised to continue on his anti-rejection treatment, monitoring the kidney and liver function; the cyclosporin level and blood glucose.

Thank you for your cooperation.

Thank you.

**Yours Sincerely,**

**PROF.DR.**████████

**Nephrologist Consultant**

**Examination:**(2005-8-3)

WBC:  13.3*10E9/L          HB: 122g/L

HCT:  36.9%                PLT: 384*10E9/L

K+:  4.13  .mmol/L         Na+:140 mmol/L

Cre:103  umol/L

(2004-8-3-CsA-TL):

C0:334ng/ml               C2:1310 ng/ml

**Suggestion:**

1, come back to native hospital to continue his treatment.

2, checking up the rejection medicine level and adjusting the dose of rejection drugs on time.

KUNMING   KIDNEY   HOSPITAL

DOCTOR ███████

2005/8/6

# MEDICAL RECORDER

**Name** ████████ **Sex:maLe** **Age:** 53y

**Blood group: B**

**Disease diagnosis**: end-stage-renal-failure

The patient was admitted to our center on June 26th 2005,. and accepted kidney transplantation on July 19th 2005, with graft renal artery end-to-side anastomosed to extensive iliac artery, the graft vein end-to-side anastomsed to extensive iliac vein, The graft ureter anastomosed to bladder. and the CyciosporineA, Cellcept, prednisone have been used to prevent rejection. After operation the volume of urine increase to about 15000ml/d. now the graft renal function recovered well, the creatinine decreased to 103umol/l. And now . the patient's condition has been getting better and been discharged from our center.

**Immunosuppressive:**

| | | |
|---|---|---|
| CsA | 160mg | 8AM/8PM |
| Cellcept: | 1g | 8AM/8PM |
| Pred: | 20mg | qd |
| Famotidine | 20mg | Bid |
| Acyclovir | 0.2g | tid |

Almost all the kidneys transplanted in China prior to 2008 came from executed prisoners as the recipients were informed regarding the source of the "donated" kidneys. Typically, the patients would wait for several days to a few weeks before suitably matched kidneys were obtained for transplantation. Post transplantation, the patients would remain between 2-4 weeks in the hospital for close observation, removal of surgical drains, ureteric stent and urinary catheter before they were discharged to continue further care in their home country.

While many Malaysian patients with end stage renal failure who went to China came back with a successful and uncomplicated transplantation, others faced harrowing ordeals including mortal outcomes in China itself or after returning home.

For the fortunate ones that returned home alive with uncomplicated surgery, satisfactory allograft outcome and excellent post transplant progress, they would enjoy the promised improvement in clinical status and quality of life. The rest, unfortunately, faced varying degrees of clinical complications and socio-economic difficulties. These included acute rejections, some were steroid resistant requiring expensive second line anti-rejection therapy (typically ATG or Thymoglobulin for 5-7 days), systemic bacterial infections including life threatening pneumonia and septicaemia occasionally requiring ventilatory and intensive care support while others encountered significant systemic fungal infections and viral infections including Hepatitis B and Hepatitis C.

As the transplant recipients could no longer afford to travel to the respective transplant centres in China, they had to rely on public hospitals in their home country for assistance and further treatment.

In the run up to the 2008 Beijing Olympics and under closer scrutiny from the watchful eyes and pressure from the international community, it became clearer that the so called "legal" and "ethical" transplants in China were not so legal and ethical after all. The syndicates operating these illegal networks had to be more vigilant to protect and hide their heinous activities from the arms of the suspecting and more responsible Chinese authorities to avoid possible disruption to the planned and prestigious Beijing Olympics. The syndicates would, by then, arrange for potential transplant recipients to be kept away from the actual operating centres until a suitable date could be secured. Post-surgery, the patients would have to be quickly bundled out of the hospital to prevent the authorities from sniffing out their illegal activities (see case 3 which follows). In addition to avoiding detection by the regulatory authorities, it would be arranged for the patient to return home earlier to avoid mounting bills so as to retain the profit margin.

In 2006, the first evidence of such hurried and anonymous procedures became evident when a patient returned home a week after transplant with a urinary catheter in situ, despite absence of urine for a day prior to his discharge. The unfortunate patient referred himself to a public hospital near the capital for an emergency treatment immediately after his arrival at the Kuala Lumpur airport. Difficulty and dilemma occurred at the emergency department as there was no accompanying customary referral letter from the transplant centre in China to indicate the type of procedures performed, the progress, laboratory results and treatment, including medications post transplantation. An emergency duplex ultrasound and cystoscopy had to be arranged, the results of which confirmed that the patient had suffered from an anastomotic breakdown of the transplant ureter which required urgent surgical repair.

Even though the number of renal transplant patients returning from China had dwindled significantly since 2006 (see table 1), the management of such patients became, unfortunately, more complicated and challenging. The main reason for this circumstance was due to the fact that ALL new returning transplant recipients from China since 2006 no longer brought along with them any form of documentation to guide the clinicians in Malaysia to provide optimal follow-up care. Such a practice is, in part, a deliberate attempt by the syndicate members to remain anonymous, unacountable and to leave absolutely no trace of their illegal activities. However, the absence of any information on the perioperative as well as postoperative findings, clinical summary, necessary information on the type and dose of the induction agents given, the best serum allograft function achieved and the lack of many other standard test results had caused a serious gap in the ability of the local clinicians to deliver a quality and effective care deserved by such patients who had not only risked their lives and parted with their hard earned life savings to obtain a new, safer and better quality of life but now faced real and potentially serious transplant related complications.

Table 1: Renal transplants in Malaysian patients performed in China and India.

| Country/Year | 2001 | 2002 | 2003 | 2004 | 2005 | 2006 | 2007 | 2008 | 2009 | 2010 |
|---|---|---|---|---|---|---|---|---|---|---|
| China | 83 | 103 | 111 | 139 | 110 | 87 | 45 | 63 | 58 | 35 |
| India | 8 | 12 | 4 | 11 | 7 | 7 | 3 | 3 | 1 | 1 |

Source: 18th Malaysian Dialysis and Transplant Registry (MDTR)

Statistics reported by the Malaysian Dialysis and Transplant Registry not only showed the persistence of commercial kidney transplant activities after the conclusion of the Beijing Olympics in 2008, but also that the syndicates had changed tactics to remain elusive and hide from the hands of the Chinese authorities. More importantly, they had also started focusing on a new source of organ donation. The report issued by MDTR in 2011 (table 2) clearly showed the increasing trend of commercial live kidney donors as opposed to commercial deceased donor kidney transplants in Malaysian patients returning from the People's Republic of China after 2008.

Table 2: Type of kidney donor for transplants performed in China involving Malaysian patients 2004-2010

| Year/Type of donor | 2004 | 2005 | 2006 | 2007 | 2008 | 2009 | 2010 |
|---|---|---|---|---|---|---|---|
| Commercial deceased donor | 145 | 107 | 85 | 45 | 60 | 33 | 8 |
| Commercial live donor | 6 | 9 | 8 | 4 | 2 | 20 | 20 |

Source: 18th Malaysian Dialysis and Transplant Registry (MDTR)

The following real-life cases exemplify the clinical risks and challenges arising from the organ trafficking and organ trading faced by patients from Malaysia.

**Case 1** Mr. CC, a 35-year old luxury car trader with an unknown cause of end stage kidney disease, went to China in 2009 for a commercial unrelated renal transplant after 6 months of hemodialysis treatment. He appeared well when he returned to Kuala Lumpur 3 weeks after the seemingly successful transplant. The overseas transplant trip costed him USD 50,000.

At the first encounter in his home city, laboratory tests for his graft function and liver functions were normal. A month later, his liver enzymes suddenly increased tenfold. This was attributed to acute Hepatitis B when the serology for the viral antigen, which was negative at the first clinic encounter, became positive. Further complication occurred as he developed significant biopsy proven acute allograft rejection following temporary modification of his immunosuppressive medications during the phase of acute Hepatitis B infection. While the acute rejection was responsive to pulse intravenous steroid treatment, his Hepatitis B viral infection unfortunately persisted in the next 2 years requiring further treatment and follow up causing much anguish and uncertainty. While cases of post transplant Hepatitis B infection are uncommon, in contrast, infection with Hepatitis C in transplant patients returning from China is unfortunately not so infrequent.

**Case 2** Mr. AD exemplified a case involving a patient who was transplanted without regard to the safety and appropriateness of performing such a major surgical procedure without adequate preoperative investigations and preparation. The 56 year old gentleman with end stage kidney disease due to complications of diabetes mellitus returned to Malaysia two weeks after having a live unrelated commercial renal transplant in Southern China. More than USD 60,000 changed hands before a suitable kidney was sourced from a young Chinese male. The transplant recipient experienced several episodes of chest pains after the transplant surgery attributed to previously undiagnosed coronary artery disease. Upon his return, he experienced recurrent chest pain resulting in hypotension and functional deterioration of his transplanted kidney. A full blown heart attack ensued which led to a complete shutdown of his transplant kidney function. More complications followed after he required ventilatory and continuous dialysis support as his kidney allograft had failed. He eventually succumbed after a week of intensive care without ever regaining consciousness.

The third case clearly illustrates the clandestine nature of the syndicate operatives.

**Case 3** Dr. FA was a 55 year old medical administrator in a public hospital. He was on hemodialysis for 4 years before he was assisted by a racketeer in travelling to Southern China with another friend who also had kidney failure. They were promised a kidney transplant after paying a deposit of USD 30,000 each. Upon arrival, he was kept in a budget hotel and had his hemodialysis arranged at a private hemodialysis unit. After a week of waiting, he was told to get ready to move to a "hospital" as a suitable live donor was finally found. He was perplexed as his transfer was arranged under cover of darkness. From the "hospital" bed he was subsequently moved to another location in the early hours of the next morning for the actual "transplant". Unfortunately, after waiting for a few hours in an isolation room in the new "hospital", he was told by an interpreter that the transplant surgery had to be cancelled at the last minute as the surgeons faced some "unexpected obstacles" from a few visitors. He was hurriedly packed into a car to be moved back to his hotel. It was then revealed to him by his interpreter that his friend did undergo two transplant surgeries, under dubious circumstances, the second one apparently offered at no additional cost after the immediate failure of the first transplant surgery. Sniffing something seriously wrong and fearing for his life, he decided to return home and continued his fully subsidised hemodiafiltration treatment in his home state.

Given the complexity, sensitivity and emotive nature of overseas transplant subjects in a country with inherently a low organ donation rate together with the need to abide by the WHO Guiding Principles on Human Cell, Tissue and Organ Transplantation and Istanbul Declaration On Transplant Commercialism, Malaysian health authorities embarked on a two-pronged strategy in an attempt to stem or discourage the flow of Malaysian patients seeking illegal organ transplants overseas, namely:

1. By strengthening local resources and public awareness to increase organ donation rate in the country and,

2. By creating a policy of disincentive by withdrawal of free supply of expensive immunosuppressive medications to recipients of such organs from illegal sources.

Responsible professionals in the country would continue to remain vigilant to ensure that not only an appropriate and legal organ transplant program which conforms to the highest professional and universal ethical standard shall flourish in this country and this region, but also that the practice to the contrary will not be tolerated and will be resisted by all possible means.

---

1  Laimy Boey. Nursing Sister, Renal Transplant Unit. Dept of Nephrology, Hospital Kuala Lumpur.

2  Malaysian Dialysis and Transplant Registry.

# How Many Harvested?

## A Survey-based Estimate of Falun Gong Murdered from 2000 to 2008

ETHAN GUTMANN

As this chapter goes to the final edit, Chinese medical authorities have just announced the intent to end organ harvesting of death-row prisoners within five years, and a sort of nervous euphoria is sweeping across the Falun Gong community.[1] Among those practitioners who have relations, friends and comrades incarcerated throughout China, it is hoped, and fervently desired, that Beijing's decision will apply to prisoners of conscience as well – and yet, no mention of political and religious prisoners was made in the announcement, not in the Chinese press, not even in the Western free press. Everyone understands which lines can be safely crossed; this is not one of them. So the taboo holds, at least for now, even though it requires a conscious act of doublethink to avoid the thoughtcrime: the shift in policy is driven by fear – not Beijing's humanitarian concern over exploiting the death of murderers and rapists, but a rapidly-congealing sense of dread at the prospect that the Chinese Communist Party's historic crime will be laid bare before the world – and worse, before the Chinese people.

The timing of recent developments – so inextricably enmeshed in the current Chinese leadership struggle over succession – is instructive. In November 2011, the Chinese medical establishment published an article in the respected British medical journal *Lancet*.[2] Entitled "A pilot programme of organ donation after cardiac death in China," the article could fairly be characterized as a vague apologia for China's unethical transplant environment, the equivalent of a series of promissory notes to do better, and some baseline harvesting numbers. The latter were clearly improvised rather than a genuine tabulation; in fact, the numbers already exhibited a dramatic and unexpected diminishing of prisoners being harvested as a percentage of transplants. Predictably the authors preemptively reject any independent verification, and we can safely assume that the figures will undoubtedly show stunning progress towards a more ethical transplant environment in the near future.

If the *Lancet* article was a seedling, it was followed by the sudden blossoming of a crisis over the ongoing case of Wang Lijun, formerly the chief of the Public Security Bureau of Jinzhou City and a protégé of Bo Xilai, (the recently-demoted candidate for the Politburo Standing Committee). In the wake of Wang's recent attempt to defect at the American Consulate in Chengdu, his true role has emerged as an overseer of "several thousand intensive on-site cases" of transplantation in 2006. At an awards ceremony for medical innovation, Wang openly proclaimed that he found the act of observing execution followed by transplant to be "soul-stirring".[3] Could we expect any less coming from Wang – or for that matter, Bo Xilai? Both men built a measure of their political capital on the ruthless repression of Falun Gong.[4] Such are the rites of passage, the leadership qualifications that the Party demands, and yet, in a leadership conflict, the old rules can quickly turn. Bo Xilai mobilized armored fighting vehicles to pressure the American Consulate in Chengdu.[5] A few weeks later the Chinese microblogs were rife with rumors of tanks (presumably moving against Bo's faction) on the streets in Beijing.[6] At the same time, certain blocked web searches became available on Beidu most notably those pertaining to "live organ harvesting".[7] A few days later, Huang Jiefu, China's Vice Minister of Health, made the public declaration of intent to end organ donations from executed prisoners within three to five years. And while all these events transpire, the master architect of the repression of Falun Gong, Jiang Zemin, lies at the point of death.[8]

There are many ways of interpreting these actions. Yet the one that makes the most intuitive sense is that the Party has decided to sponge away organ harvesting and the most damaging portions of its history. All the factors are in place: a promissory note that avoids the main subject (the *Lancet* article), a couple of scapegoats (Bo Xilai and Wang Lijun) to deflect responsibility from the Party leadership, a game of chicken between factions (played out with tanks and on the Internet), and waiting in the wings, a dying leader ready to absorb any excess guilt (in the standard formulation – Jiang could be declared to be 70% right and 30% wrong). Indeed, for the survival of the Party, the only way to stop harvesting of prisoners of conscience is to deny that it has ever existed and to simultaneously bury any remaining evidence of what has occurred over the last fifteen years.

Given this scenario, I do not believe that any of us who have worked on the issue can declare victory until the Party allows a comprehensive, transparent, on-the-ground investigation into the harvesting of political and religious prisoners – Uighurs, Falun Gong, Tibetans, and House Christians – from 1997 to 2012. It is imperative for many, many voices to join us in that demand. Yet, quite understandably, few will do so until they begin to grapple with the scale of the crime.

Ironically, the first step towards achieving that external interest and support is to admit how provisional our findings are and explain how severe are the limitations we operate under. This is how I stated the problem back in 2009:

> Indeed, the entire investigation must be understood to be still at an early, even primitive, stage. We do not really know the scale of what is happening yet. Think of 1820, when a handful of doctors, scientists, and amateur fossil hunters were trying to make sense of scattered suggestive evidence and a disjointed pile of bones. Twenty-two years would pass before an English paleontologist so much as coined the term "dinosaur" – "terrible lizard" – and the modern study of these extinct creatures got seriously under way. Those of us researching the harvesting of organs from involuntary donors in China are like the early dinosaur hunters. We don't work in close consultation with each other. We are still waiting for even one doctor who has harvested organs from living prisoners of conscience to emerge from the mainland. Until that happens, it is true, we don't even have dinosaur bones.[9]

The main point is still relevant – trying to see into the unmarked compounds of China is like examining a star. Any light we can see has already occurred and our assumptions about the present hinge on faint radio signals over time. Yet, I am also repeating my statement to suggest how far we have come.

The first medical witnesses have emerged from their corners in exile. A surgeon has spoken – on the record and in great personal detail – of harvesting a living human being on an execution ground in 1995.[10] A medical intern has recounted his participation in the blood-testing of Uighur political prisoners on behalf of Chinese Communist Party officials waiting for kidney and liver transplants in 1997.[11] We have bones, and as new witnesses emerge from the Tibetan and Uighur communities, we have a broader landscape for excavation. Simultaneously the investigation into the harvesting of Falun Gong practitioners, the bulk of the organ supply, has evolved beyond the initial witnesses – the opaque motives of "Peter" and "Annie" and the occasionally ambiguous phone conversations with mainland doctors – into increasingly solid confirmation.[12] A former prisoner, a non-practitioner, gave an explicit account to Kilgour and Matas of a Falun Gong prisoner being prepared for organ removal.[13] A respected Taiwanese surgeon confessed to me, with no small measure of shame and embarrassment, that his patients were regular recipients of Falun Gong organs on the mainland.[14]

For some readers these facts may be new and shocking. But the references are readily available. Should we wait for widespread Western indifference and denial to catch up with the facts? We have amassed enough evidence and gathered enough of a consensus that a book such as this has finally become possible, and, while it will undoubtedly see revision, we now have the beginning of the story.

Live organ harvesting of prisoners was pioneered in 1994. The first Uighur political prisoners were harvested, at least on a small scale, in 1997 following the Ghulja Incident in Xinjiang.[15] The first Falun Gong practitioners were harvested in the latter half of 2000, although harvesting of Falun Gong on a mass scale (including a presently unknown number of Tibetans and House Christian sects such as "Eastern Lightning") did not begin in earnest until autumn of 2002. Harvesting peaked in 2006 to 2007, prematurely forced into a close-of-business sale by the first, seminal articles in the *Epoch Times* on harvesting and the subsequent Kilgour-Matas report.[16]

We are far from writing an end to the story. There are clear cases of practitioners being examined for potential harvesting after 2006, despite the Chinese leadership's desire for a scandal-free Beijing Olympics. The question of Falun Gong being harvested after 2008 is still open. There are also extraordinary numbers of Tibetan and Uighur activists missing in the wake of their respective uprisings in 2008 and 2009. And yet, we have a special obligation to investigate the high volume period, specifically the organ harvesting of Falun Gong between 2000, the point when the wide-scale incarceration of practitioners became a permanent fixture and 2008, the point at which harvesting retracted, and I believe our evidence becomes less reliable.

The reason for examining and debating such numbers boils down to human instinct. As a survival mechanism of our species, we must contextualize, evaluate, and ultimately learn from every human descent into mass murder and genocide. Counting the dead is one tool in our arsenal, a tool that can be used for placing the trauma in historical context. Westerners, perhaps unavoidably, employ the Holocaust as our ultimate benchmark of genocide. Chinese might intuitively make comparisons with the Nanjing Massacre and Unit 731, Japan's wartime human experimental program. Either way, I will return to these comparisons very briefly at the end of this chapter.

I employ a survey method based on my interviews. As I signaled in the beginning, gauging the scale of prisoners of conscience who were fatally exploited for their retail organs is problematic and probably will be for years to come. So I have generated a provisional solution, a placeholder, an alternate method to Kilgour and Matas' seminal research until the second wave of bones – the sort of information that Wang Lijun was privy to – is revealed.

A word about methodology and motivation – as a former business consultant in Beijing, I carry a deep-rooted distrust of Chinese official numbers. I used to advise my corporate clients that even if they are looking at tapioca production figures, mainland numbers are often coded political messages that only reflect reality selectively. Having said that, Kilgour and Matas made their calculations of Falun Gong harvested working off of figures that emerged before there was extreme political sensitivity regarding the topic. At times, Kilgour and Matas were privately disparaged because there was variance in their Chinese sources on the number of organs harvested over time. Yet to my mind, that very lack of consistency suggests that the numbers might not be Party-driven propaganda. So in short, I don't reject official numbers or methods of analysis that use them, but I instinctively look for other ways to get at the information, if only to serve as a point of comparison.

I have been writing about Falun Gong since 2002.[17] In 2006, when the organ harvesting allegations emerged, I was open-minded, but I preserved what I believed to be an appropriate level of skepticism. Organ harvesting or not, I was firmly convinced that a comprehensive account of the conflict between the Chinese State and Falun Gong was overdue, and I began a lengthy interview process to fill that gap. One of my very first interviews was in Toronto with three women who were fresh out of labor camp. Even in that early stage, I recognized that their stories were relatively routine – Tiananmen demonstrations followed by incarceration and the usual attempts at "transformation" (forcing the practitioners to reject Falun Gong): torture, brainwashing, and humiliation. One of the women, (let's call her "Wang" to protect her family) was the least articulate but had a very appealing salt-of-the-earth quality to her. At one point she mentioned a "funny" physical exam in passing. I asked Wang to explain. She did not consider the matter important and wanted to go on with her real story. I persisted – had she been hunger striking? No. Was anyone else examined? Yes, some other Falun Gong. What were the tests? A urine sample, a large blood test, an EKG, some tapping around the stomach and groin, x-rays, and then the doctor spent a lot of time shining a light into her eyes. Was there a peripheral vision test? No. A reading test? No. A vision test, anything involving actual seeing? No. Was there any test of her ears, nose or her throat? Her genitals, her reflexes? No. In fact there was nothing that could constitute a proper physical examination. The tests were aimed at the health of Wang's liver, kidneys, heart, and corneas – the retail organs.

Wang had no clear idea of the implications of what she was relating and was slightly irritated at my Western inability to see the woods for the trees – the woods, in this case, being her spiritual battle. While I didn't believe that Wang had been seriously considered as a candidate for organ harvesting – probably too old – some of the other women that had received the same examinations as Wang almost certainly were – and I remember feeling a chill as my safe, hedging cloak of skepticism fell away.

I don't intend to reproduce that chill for the reader of this chapter. But my skepticism never returned, in part because after a number of interviews that followed a similar pattern of targeted physical examination, I was working with evidence of organ harvesting that I could put my arms around. Over several years I interviewed over 100 subjects, some interviews lasting for several days, in a process that ranged across four continents. A majority of my subjects had experienced some form of detention. Fifty of my subjects were Falun Gong refugees from labor camps, prisons and long-term detention facilities. Of these, 16 were subjected to suspicious medical testing.[18]

Clearly 50 subjects would be a statistical trifle in most consumer studies, but wartime studies and intelligence operations often have to make do with far less. It's not a purely random sample – I spent an evening in Bangkok actively seeking out a practitioner who had experienced unusual medical examinations – but my method was not a push-poll in any sense. My research interests encompass a vast array of subjects within Falun Gong's history, so Bangkok was counterbalanced by Hong Kong, Taipei, and extensive interviews across North America, Europe and Australia where my selection process favored practitioners who had direct experience of Falun Gong's rise in the Nineties or of the early days of the crackdown. Most of these practitioners served relatily short sentences by current standards and were released before organ harvesting became common.[19] Yet in acknowledgement of the sample size, I try to avoid trying to fix a single number of fatalities from organ harvesting – which skeptics might justifiably seize on as an example of false precision – in favor of establishing a plausible range of fatalities and constructing a "best-guess" or a middle number from that range.

To begin, we must have some basic agreement about the overall numbers of prisoners in China. One option is to use the U.S. State Department's number of 250,000, essentially a number chosen from one of the Party's published summaries of total inmates in the country's re-education-through-labor camps.[20] Human rights groups (and somewhat ironically, the U.S. State Department's own Bureau of Democracy, Human Rights, and Labor) commonly use a labor camp estimate of 400,000 to 500,000.[21] Yet all of these figures ultimately can be traced back to Chinese government sources and the only reason the Chinese publish them is to propagate an idea: China is humane, incarcerating its citizens at a rate far below most of the world, (approximately seven times less than the U.S., for example).[22]

The other option is to think about the entire network of prisons, jails, labor camps (*Laogai*), detention centers, black jails and psychiatric institutions that the Laogai Research Foundation refers to as the *Laogai System* – a definition that captures the real-life experiences of Falun Gong practitioners or indeed any other dissidents in China: tossed by prevailing Party winds and the currents of provincial politics from detention center or black jail to all manner of long-term incarceration. Taking into account the Laogai Research Foundation's caveat that "it is impossible to know with certainty how many inmates are imprisoned in the Laogai or how many camps exist," and even without including detention or psychiatric centers, the Laogai Research Foundation counts well over 1,000 nodes – prison and labor camp facilities throughout the mainland. They researched each location for any clues on its economic output, and then used these figures and other clues to estimate how many prisoners might be contained within it. This building-blocks approach is a legitimate and defensible method, in my opinion, and the Laogai Research Foundation currently estimates the number of prisoners in the Laogai System as 3 to 5 million.[23]

In terms of establishing a base Falun Gong population in 1999, the problem is significantly easier because I was able to interview Hao Fengjun, a former officer of the "610 Office" (the Chinese security agency created to eliminate Falun Gong). Although Falun Gong practitioners claimed figures ranging between 70 to 100 million, as did various Chinese media outlets, my personal interviews with Hao revealed that the 610 Office's internal, working estimate of Falun Gong's pre-crackdown population was 70 million.

| Baseline estimates | Low estimate | High estimate |
| --- | --- | --- |
| Total prisoners in Laogai System at any given time | 3,000,000 | 5,000,000 |
| Falun Gong base population in 1999 | 70,000,000 | 70,000,000 |

How many of the Laogai System prisoners were Falun Gong? Practitioners on the ground in China assumed that over one million Falun Gong were incarcerated in the first years of the crackdown.[24] Based on clues from my interviews, these claims had a bearing in reality, yet they came from people who had no previous experience in analyzing the Chinese penal system. Western journalists (with little experience in estimating prison populations themselves) often pointed to the fact that such claims were unsubstantiated and essentially dropped the subject. Human rights watchdog groups, Amnesty International, Human Rights Watch and Freedom House, never made a systematic attempt to generate a figure either, and no U.S. congressman requested such information with any particular urgency.

In any case, the numbers shifted over time. The Party's response to the Tiananmen demonstrations of 2000 to 2001 and the subsequent Laogai System overcrowding was to use transformation methods of increasing severity. These worked, and the amount of Falun Gong practitioners in prison rapidly declined. But the government never achieved the 99% transformation rate that it claimed. Hao believes it was closer to 50% and he points to the high rate of recidivism and, from the Party's perspective, a dangerous new militancy – leaflet distribution, banners, and Internet activity. So even if smaller numbers of Falun Gong were being arrested – for a second or third time – few were being released. They couldn't be. With the hijacking of TV signals, with the distribution of *The Nine Commentaries* throughout China, practitioners were now considered dangerous enemies of the State.[25] The repeat offenders were in far flung labor camps and with fewer practitioners in low-security, local detention centers, fewer messages were smuggled out and fewer families could make the long trip to visit their relations. As the voices of those in China's Laogai System dropped out of range, the ability of overseas practitioners to accurately analyze the scale of Falun Gong incarceration faded. Under the skeptical eye of the Western press, in 2002 the overseas Falun Gong persecution-tracking sites established the ultra-cautious number 100,000 as a low-ball, and presumably defensible, estimate of practitioners in custody.[26]

Implicitly contradicting the Falun Gong number, U.N. Special Rapporteur on Torture, Manfred Nowak, made a statement in 2009 that Falun Gong comprised fully 50% the population of China's prison camps; Nowak was apparently relying on refugee testimony and his statement was consistent with an earlier report in which he asserted that Falun Gong constituted 66% of the alleged torture cases in China.[27] Nowak's torture percentage feels intuitively accurate to me, but the 100,000 estimate and the 50% estimate cannot both be correct unless the Laogai population was 200,000 or less.

I reject both estimates. Nowak should be honored for having the courage to treat practitioner claims seriously but the fact is that in the atomized world of the Laogai, there are no practitioners in a position to make plausible system-wide estimates. In any given interview with a refugee from the Laogai System, I don't ask the subject about the overall system, but I do ask them for an accurate breakdown of the amount of practitioners within their own cellblock. Based on 50 interviews where each practitioner gave me their personal snapshot of their particular situation, I estimate that the practitioner representation in China's Laogai System averages out to about 30% of women and 10%-15% of men. Given the over-representation of men in the Laogai system, I further estimate that, on the low end, male and female practitioners collectively represent 15% of the Laogai System at any given time. On the high end, 20%. While the high estimate may have been operative in 2001 and the low estimate is more likely to have been operative in 2008, we can say that the average number of practitioners in the Laogai System at any given time ranges between 450,000 and 1,000,000.

| Falun Gong in Laogai System at any given time | Low estimate | High estimate |
|---|---|---|
| Percentage of Falun Gong in Laogai System at any given time | 15% | 20% |
| Average number of Falun Gong in Laogai System at any given time | 450,000 | 1,000,000 |

If these numbers seem high, I confess that they surprised me too at first glance. Yet, consider our starting point of 70 million. If you use the lower estimate, less than 1% of the Falun Gong base population is actually in the Laogai System at any given time. In the high estimate, it's approximately 1.5%.

The next step is to determine how many practitioners have been in the Laogai system at some point over the last nine years. Again, based on my fifty refugees, I came up with answers across the board – in the early years, a year or two in detention was common. By 2008, five year sentences were routine. A three-year term on average captures the variability with reasonable accuracy.[28]

| Total Falun Gong in Laogai System 2000 to 2008 | Low estimate | High estimate |
|---|---|---|
| Average amount of time a practitioner is in the Laogai System | 3 years | 3 years |
| Total Falun Gong in Laogai System at some point, 2000 to 2008 | 1,200,000 | 2,666,667 |

From my 50 practitioner subjects, 16 of them, or approximately 30% of my sample, received physical examinations that were in some aspect, inexplicable and incongruous other than as an assessment of organ transplant viability. Those 16, in turn, can be divided into two groups.

In the first group, I have placed 8 practitioners, or 15% of my sample, who seem to have been examined "for show" – i.e. practitioners who were obviously too old, too sick, or too weakened by hunger strike to be plausible candidates for harvesting. My theory, borne out by the signs of anxiety with which the authorities viewed these tests, (in an extreme example, an armed guard was matched up with every female practitioner) is that the "for show" practitioners were given the same examinations as every other practitioner simply to make the procedure seem normal and to keep the prisoners from panicking.

In the second group, I have placed 8 practitioners or 15% of my sample, who were younger, relatively healthy, and were not on hunger strike. Their exams differed from location to location but they invariably included these central components: blood tests, a urine test, an EKG, and x-rays of the abdomen (examination of the cornea was standard practice in 2002 but dropped by 2006). Crucially, they were then given a series of follow-up medical tests usually corresponding with tissue matching. Members of this group were candidates for harvesting.

| Falun Gong examined in Laogai System | Low estimate | High estimate |
|---|---|---|
| Percentage of Falun Gong examined in custody | 30% | 30% |
| Falun Gong examined in custody | 360,000 | 800,000 |
| Percentage of Falun Gong examined "for show" | 50% | 50% |
| Falun Gong examined as candidates for harvesting | 180,000 | 400,000 |
| Percentage of Falun Gong selected for harvesting | 5% | 30% |

What percentage of the practitioners examined for harvesting were actually selected for surgery? On the low estimate, I premise that, in spite of all the testing and the profits to be made, only 1 out of every 20 practitioners was actually selected and a selection rate lower than that strains credulity.[29] But what drives the high estimate selection number of 30%? Most practitioners in the Laogai System only had an amorphous awareness of the organ harvesting issue during their detention, yet their recollections, even in hindsight, establish that following a series of medical tests in labor camp one out of every three or four of the practitioners who had received the follow-up exams might be "relocated." It is exceedingly difficult for most practitioners to say definitively if this was an actual selection for organ harvesting. However, they were better positioned to make such an estimate than any outsider that I am aware of, so I accept their percentage as the top range.[30]

As you can see in the following chart, that, plus the accumulation of previous assumptions regarding high and low estimates leads to a wide differential. Fair enough. Given the uncertainties in the process, I have consciously tried to avoid precision where the evidence does not justify it. Yet both the low estimate and the high estimate are genuine outliers, and I don't really believe in either extreme. The truth is found somewhere in the middle and that's why I provide a median or a best estimate, 64,500, which I have rounded up to 65,000.

| Best estimate of Falun Gong harvested 2000 to 2008 | Low estimate | High estimate |
| --- | --- | --- |
| Total Falun Gong harvested 2000 to 2008 | 9,000 | 120,000 |
| "Best estimate" | 65,000 | |

So what percentage of Falun Gong has been simply eliminated? A fraction of a percentage point. As I've said previously, by Holocaust standards (and even by Nanjing standards to a lesser extent), these are piddling numbers. But 65,000 is a number that is far too big to write off as a mere aberration either. Similar to the Holocaust then, the scale of this operation required police bureaucrats and military medical personnel to become extremely creative, to build systems: of detention, of quarantine, and even of health – once a stable of blood types was created it was not in the interest of the military hospital system to let their investment depreciate. The latter imperative was counter to the spirit of the Laogai System and it required unprecedented coordination with military medical personnel. Ultimately it also required the medical side to assume responsibility for murder and disposal, and it is this procedure, not the numbers, that has attracted the most outside attention to my work.[31] It's not the fact that the Chinese state killed people who could not, even under the loose standards of Chinese law, be sentenced to death or that a majority may well have been relatively young women. It's the fact the surgery was indisputably carried out while they were still alive.[32]

Initially I found the external fascination with live organ harvesting to be misplaced, sentimental, even a cloaked form of denial. Yet I was wrong – what ties the Falun Gong harvesting atrocity to the genocide of the Holocaust (and very neatly to Unit 731) is that it required the employment of the most venerated members of society, the doctors, to carry it out. Happily then, we have fallen short in the numbers, but unfortunately we have approached Holocaust levels of medical corruption, and we have done it in our time.

Some might say that the individual Chinese doctors, such as Huang Jiefu, who penned the article in *Lancet* may be quite sincere in their desire to reform the system. I agree with them. Yet a few good intentions cannot sponge away history. If respected Western medical journals are too polite or simply too naïve to reject a laughable attempt at "obfuscation propaganda," if Western reporters are too scared to cross the invisible lines that their Chinese hosts have so clearly laid out for them, then the truth needs to be stated clearly.

What has occurred is a crime against all humanity. And yet, ironically enough, only the victims' families have the right to absolve China. Above all, no Western entity possesses the moral authority to allow the Party to bury the full history of genocide in exchange for promises of medical reform.

1 See Keith Bradsher, China Moves to Stop Transplants of Organs After Executions, *New York Times*, 23 March 2012, <nytimes. com/2012/03/24/world/asia/china-moves-to-stop-transplants-of-organs-after-executions.html?pagewanted=1&_r=1&ref=transplants>, accessed 9 April 2012; "China to end organ donations from executed prisoners," *BBC*, 23 March 2012, <bbc.co.uk/news/world-asia-china-17485103>, accessed 5 April, 2012; Laurie Burkitt, "China to Stop Harvesting Inmate Organs," *Wall Street Journal*, 23 March 2012, <online.wsj.com/article/SB100014240527023047244004577298661625345898.html>, accessed 9 April 2012. For an example of the heightened mood among Chinese practitioners see Editorial Board, "Beijing Power Struggle Heralds End of Chinese Communist Party," *Epoch Times*, 31 March 2012, ,<theepochtimes.com/n2/opinion/beijing-power-struggle-heralds-end-of-chinese-communist-party-211702.html>, accessed April 9, 2012.

2 See Jiefu Huang MD, J Michael Millis MD, Yilei Mao MD, M Andrew Millis BS, Xinting Sang MD, Shouxian Zhong MD, "A pilot programme of organ donation after cardiac death in China," *The Lancet*, Volume 379, Issue 9818, Pages 862 - 865, 3 March 2012; Published Online: 11 November 2011. A full copy is accessible at <d.dxy.cn/preview/4035884>, accessed 13 March 2012.

3 WOIPFG, "Investigative Report: China's Public Security Bureau's On-site Psychology Research Center Implicated in Live Organ Harvesting and Human Experimentation on Falun Gong Practitioners," <zhuichaguoji.org/en/node/214> , 15 February, 2012, accessed on 12 March 2012. See also Matthew Robertson, "Would-be China Defector, Once Bo Xilai's Right Hand, Oversaw Organ Harvesting," *Epoch Times*, <theepochtimes.com/n2/china-news/would-be-china-defector-once-bo-xilai-s-right-hand-oversaw-organ-harvesting-191338.html>, 15 February 2012, accessed 12 March 2012.

4   Stephen Gregory, "Rewarded for Torture: The Rise of Bo Xilai in China," *Epoch Times*, <theepochtimes.com/n2/china-news/rewarded-for-torture-the-rise-of-bo-xilai-in-china-204452-all.html> March 13, 2012, accessed March 17, 2012.

5   Bill Gertz, "Defection Denied," *Washington Free Beacon*, 26 March 2012, <freebeacon.com/defection-denied/>, accessed 9April 2012.

6   "Crackdown in China after Coup Rumours" *The Statesman*, 31 March 2012, <thestatesman.net/index.php?option=com_content&view=article&id=405043&catid=35>, accessed 9April 2012.

7   Matthew Robertson, "Chinese Internet Allows Searches for 'Live (Organ) Harvest'," 26 March 2012, <theepochtimes.com/n2/china-news/chinese-internet-allows-searches-for-live-organ-harvest-210507.html>, accessed 9April 2012.

8   Po Hui'er, "Former Chinese Regime Leader Jiang Zemin Said to Be in Vegetative State," *Epoch Times*, 26 March  2012, <theepochtimes.com/n2/china-news/former-party-leader-jiang-said-to-be-on-life-support-210916.html>, accessed 9April 2012.

9   Ethan Gutmann, "China's Gruesome Organ Harvest," *Weekly Standard*, 24 November 2008.

10  Ethan Gutmann, "The Xinjiang Procedure," *Weekly Standard* 5 December 2011.

11  Gutmann, "The Xinjiang Procedure."

12  For full phone records see World Organization to Investigate the Persecution of Falun Gong (WOIPFG), "List of Hospitals and Transplant Centers in China Confirmed by WOIPFG to Harvest Organs for Transplant Operations from Living Falun Gong Practitioners," <www.zhuichaguoji.org/en/node/187>, 21 August 2008, accessed on 12 March , 2011. When I interviewed the practitioner who made the majority of the investigative calls, she asserted that the *Epoch Times* decision to expose the Sujiatun story early in 2006 dramatically interfered with both her hit rate (in terms of hospitals which were harvesting Falun Gong) and the candor of the doctors that she was able to engage. It's also germane that Laogai Research Foundation Harry Wu, originally the most prominent skeptic of the Falun Gong organ harvesting allegations (specifically over doubts about the credibility of "Annie" and "Peter") appears to have significantly modified his stance based on more recent evidence. This shift is reflected in the Laogai Research Foundation's publication of  Nicole Kempton and Nan Richardson (editors), Laogai: The Machinery of Repression in China, (Umbrage: 2009), p. 110.

13  See reference to prisoner "Lanny" in David Matas, "Organ harvesting of Falun Gong Practitioners in China: An Update," Remarks prepared for the Transplantation Society Congress, Sydney Australia, <organharvestinvestigation.net/events/D_Matas_081408.htm>, 14 August, 2008, accessed on 12 March, 2012.

14  Ethan Gutmann, "China's Policies Toward Spiritual Movements," Congressional-Executive Commission on China Roundtable discussion, <cecc.gov/pages/roundtables/2010/20100618/gutmannTestimony.pdf> 18 June, 2010, accessed on 12 March, 2012.

15  Gutmann, "The Xinjiang Procedure."

16  "Worse Than Any Nightmare: Journalist Quits China to Expose Concentration Camp Horrors and Bird Flu Coverup," *Epoch Times*, 10 March 2006; David Matas and David Kilgour, "Report into Allegations of Organ Harvesting of Falun Gong Practitioners in China," <organharvestinvestigation.net/report0607/report060706-eng. pdf>, 6 July 2006, accessed 17 March 2012; see also Gutmann, "China's Gruesome Organ Harvest."

17  Ethan Gutmann, "Who Lost China's Internet?" *Weekly Standard*, 14 February 2002. See also Ethan Gutmann, Losing the New China (Encounter, 2004), chapter 3 "MTV for War."

18  See Gutmann, "China's Gruesome Organ Harvest" for detailed case studies of key subjects.

19  My interviewees not only survived, but were able to leave China. In many cases they were able to acquire passports. That fact suggests that they came from a relatively privileged class. Not one Falun Gong practitioner that I interviewed was illiterate for example, although it's a fact that some practitioners from the country can't read. In short, my sample was slightly skewed towards those who had initiative and some form of social status. In addition, many well-known practitioners were unlikely to be candidates for organ harvesting because their detention had already become an international issue. For example in the case of Zhao Ming, Trinity College in Dublin was actively agitating for his release, and the press attention to his case was high.

20  International Religious Freedom Report 2007, East Asia and the Pacific, Bureau of Democracy, Human Rights, and Labor, <state.gov/g/drl/rls/ irf/2007/90133.htm> , accessed: 15 March, 2012.

21  See, for example, T. Kumar Advocacy Director Asia & Pacific Amnesty International USA, Amnesty International Testimony Human Rights in China And UN's Universal Periodic Review Before Tom Lantos Human Rights Commission Committee on Foreign Affairs United States Congress on January 27, 2009. For the State Department, see China (includes Tibet,

Hong Kong, and Macau) Country Reports on Human Rights Practices, Bureau of Democracy, Human Rights, and Labor, East Asia and the Pacific, March 11, 2008 <.state.gov/g/drl/rls/hrrpt/2007/100518.htm> , accessed: February 4, 2009.

22 No matter how the Party came up with such figures, they don't jibe with anything else that we know about the system. For example, China's long-term execution rate, even low-balled at 8000 per year, has been reliably estimated to be twenty times the rest of the world combined. See "China's secret execution rate revealed", *Globe and Mail*, 28 February 2006.

23 The Laogai number has actually been reduced from a previous estimate of 4-6 million. Laogai Foundation Researcher Nicole Kempton explained the reasons for the shift to me and I have reflected that change in my talks, comments to press and in my previous web-published estimates. On the latter, see <eastofethan.com>, specifically "How many harvested?" and links to updates).

24 From the end of 2000 to early 2001, practitioners may have briefly constituted the majority of all Chinese citizens incarcerated by the state. Beginning in January 2000, over 150,000 practitioners made their way to Tiananmen Square to protest. A practitioner identified as "Angel" ran a set of apartments as a practitioner staging point, occupancy ranged well into the hundreds at all times and Angel was aware of four mirror operations in the Beijing area. A short clip of intercepted police surveillance footage of Tiananmen found in the New Tang Dynasty tape archive in New York shows literally hundreds of practitioners surging into the northwest quadrant of Tiananmen Square. According to a labor camp director that I interviewed, the corresponding surge of Falun Gong (not just from Tiananmen but from all corners of China) into the prisons and labor camps in 2000-2001 was equally vivid.

25 On the hijacking incidents, see Ethan Gutmann, "Into Thin Airwaves," *Weekly Standard*, 6 December 2010.

26 WOIPFG, Announcement of the Establishment of the "Committee to Investigate the Crimes of Chinese Labor 'Re-Education' Camps in the Persecution of Falun Gong," Feb. 14, 2003. By 2007, the Falun Dafa Information Center settled on the number of 3000 practitioners killed or tortured to death although internally the suspicion was that the number was closer to 30,000. See Falun Dafa Information Center, "Persecution: Killings," <faluninfo.net/topic/6/> accessed February 4, 2012.

27 Malcolm Moore, "Seven key dates for China in 2009," *Telegraph*, <blogs.telegraph.co.uk/news/malcolmmoore/6111877/Seven_key_

dates_for_China_in_2009/ > 2 January 2009, accessed 4 February, 2012); United States Department of State, "2007 Country Reports on Human Rights Practices - China (includes Tibet, Hong Kong, and Macau)," 11 March 2008, available at <unhcr.org/cgi-bin/texis/vtx/refworld/rwmain?page=search&docid=47d92c29c8&skip=0&query=falun%20nowak > accessed 15 March 2012.

28  The assumption is that organ harvesting of prisoners of conscience was halted throughout 2008, the year of the Beijing Olympics. The "replacement rate" multiplier used here is 2.6666 rather than 3 to reflect the fact that I am counting 8 years of Falun Gong in the Laogai System (from 2000 to the end of 2007) rather than nine years. To give some perspective on these numbers: Over a nine year period, 1 out of every 52 practitioners served time in the Laogai system at some point. Using the high estimate, it's about 1 in 23.

29  Although it is not commonly understood in the West, the Chinese military, and their associated hospitals are permitted, and even officially encouraged, to act as capitalist enterprises. At the same time, physical examinations and advance testing of the sort that the practitioners describe were quite extraordinary in a labor camp setting, and incurred associated costs, chiefly surrounding equipment and deprecation. The procedure was not exactly risk-free either; Chinese organ harvesting of prisoners of conscience clearly received a nod of approval from above—it had to, because the military hospitals are under intense surveillance—but the program itself was just as clearly meant to be hidden, not only from the outside world but from the Chinese public. Having spoken to surgeons and medical personnel who have been directly involved, it is clear that harvesting of Falun Gong exists in a space that is neither legal or illegal. For example, there was no central database of practitioners and other candidates for harvesting; the doctors selected them through a system that more closely resembled eBay—not a black market exactly, but a very grey one. Like the massive counterfeiting industry which is officially condemned by the Chinese government, but not truly enforced in great swaths of China, kickbacks and pay-offs are part of the price of doing business. In counterfeiting the profits must be high enough to justify the risks, and according to at least one counterfeiting expert I knew in China, the rule of thumb was that the profit rate had to be at least 50% or it wasn't worth the trouble. To keep the organ harvesting system profitable, commensurate with the level of risk, a minimum number of practitioners needed to be harvested. For example examining one practitioner "for show" might cost approximately the equivalent of USD 100, while examining one practitioner for harvesting, might cost out at about USD 500 over time. The value of a single harvest was about USD 25,000 on average (minus 50% overhead, kickbacks, etc.). Thus if

one assumes that the costs that I'm premising are reasonably accurate, (and at least one former surgeon believes they are ball-park), and one looks at the value of total Falun Gong harvested (USD 117,000,000 on the low end with all the costs of examinations removed), to achieve a profit margin of just over 50%, practitioners had to be harvested at a rate of 5% (or one out of 20).

30 Several practitioners were convinced that there were what might be termed "mobile stables" of practitioners representing an assortment of blood types, who were harvested for foreigners and Party members. Comprised mainly of hardcore "non-transformables" and "nameless ones"—those who refused to give their names or addresses to the authorities—these practitioners were quarantined and were only seen briefly as they were shuttled through the Laogai System on their way to the military hospitals. Approximately 25% of the Falun Gong Laogai System refugees mentioned a large camp, possibly home to a million or more hard-core, "non-transformable" Falun Gong practitioners, located in north-west China. Several explicitly remember guards brandishing it as a threat: "If you don't behave, we will send you to the northwest." I was able to partially verify this claim; Alim Seytoff of the Uighur-American association confirmed that there is a camp of about 50,000 prisoners, comprised of Uighurs, Falun Gong, and hard-core criminals located in the Tarim desert, Xinjiang. All these impressions are extremely valuable, particularly for setting up a geographical reconstruction of organ harvesting centered around Shenyang Province, and although they might seem to bolster the case for a higher percentage of selection, I feel that they are too anecdotal at this time to include in the calculations.

31 See discussion of "The Xinjiang Procedure" in David Brooks, "The Sidney Awards, Part II," New York Times, December 22, 2011.

32 See Gutmann, "The Xinjiang Procedure," and "China's Gruesome Organ harvest."

# Organ Transplantation Issues in China

## ERPING ZHANG

### Chinese Culture and Organ Donation

The practice of organ transplantation in China is believed to have begun in the 1970s,[1] although such medical procedure was first successfully performed back in 1954 in Boston, USA, involving a kidney transplant between identical twins. Throughout the 5,000 year Chinese history, organ transplantation had not been formally recorded in medical documents, except some miraculous healing performed by a deity-like doctor, Bian Que (700 B.C.), in fictional stories, until some forty years ago. In fact, back then, organ transplantation was not only medically unlikely, but culturally implausible as well. As far back as the Spring and Autumn Period (771 B.C. to 476 B.C.), Confucius stated, "One's body, hair, and skin come from parents; they ought not be damaged – this is the starting point of filial piety".[2] One is supposed to keep his/her physical body in its entirety from birth to death or to the earthly burial. In the "Book of Zhou Rituals" from Western Zhou Dynasty (1046 B.C. to 771 B.C.), it was clearly stated, "All sentient beings will die and should return to the earth as a whole for peace".[3] For centuries, Chinese people have been observing this ancient belief, even to this day. Such belief has apparently proven counter-productive to the modern cause of voluntary organ donations from the public, a practice that is widely and culturally accepted in many parts of the world, Western countries in particular. Jiefu Huang, China's Vice Minister of Health, apparently recognized this when he

"... listed four reasons behind the shortfall of organ donations. 'Social custom is one of the big reasons,' he said, adding that many Chinese are unwilling to donate organs because of traditional rituals and beliefs. Furthermore, public education about donations is lacking. Another reason is the lack of a legal infrastructure".[4]

## Organ Donation Legislation

On October 9, 1984, China's Supreme Court, the Supreme People's Procuratorate of China, Ministry of Public Security, Ministry of Justice, Ministry of Health and Ministry of Civil Affairs jointly issued "Provisionary Regulations of Using Corpses and Organs from Executed Prisoners," which stated that medical institutions may utilize the unclaimed corpses and organs from executed prisoners or with consent of relatives of the executed prisoners. It has remained a concern over the years whether such consent has been properly secured, namely, on a voluntary basis, or secured at all from either the executed prisoners or from their family members. In the midst of the highly publicized allegations from the international communities about China's large-scale organ removal from Falun Gong detainees amongst other organ transplantation abuses, China's State Council issued "Human Organ Transplantation Regulations" in March 2007, which provided additional legal foundation for organ transplantation and supervision. This document was designed with the intention to ban organ trade and to prohibit foreign organ transplantation tourism to China, in light of increasing pressure and criticisms around the world.[5] On April 18, 2011, China Ministry of Health issued "Notice on Further Strengthening Human Organ Transplantation Supervision", which called for removal of medical license of doctors who violate the rules. According to a report on March 22, 2012, by Xinhua, the state-run news agency, China's State Council plans to amend the "Human Organ Transplantation Regulations" in 2012 with the clause of "encouraging citizens to donate their organs after death".[6] Yet, it remains to be seen if and when the amendment will be made in 2012 and how such regulations will be implemented.

## Reality of Organ Donation in China

Given the lack of an active voluntary donor system in China as a result of the cultural barrier, the supply of organs for transplantation has become a grave concern in China while the demand has been on the rise. As noted by Huang Jiefu, China's Vice Minister of Health, who spoke on March 22, 2012, at the China Organ Donor Work Conference, "Our country should set up an organ donation system as soon as possible so as to, within three to five years, avoid relying on the odd method of snatching organs from prisoners condemned to death".[7] At the same conference, Gao Xiang, Vice Chairman of Zhejiang Province Organ Donation Committee and Vice Chairman of Zhejiang Province Red Cross, pointed out, "our country is 150 to 1, comparing with 5 to 1 and 3 to 1 in the United States and the United Kingdom respectively, in terms of the ratio of organ recipients in waiting to organ donors".[8] According to Minister Huang's presentation "Tomorrow's Organ Transplantation Program in China" at the Madrid Conference on Organ Donation and Transplantation in 2010, " ... over 90% of grafts from deceased donors are from executed prisoners". For the past two decades, the practice of taking organs from executed prisoners has become a disturbing issue that is frequently brought up by the press, human rights groups, and medical communities around the world, even by China's domestic press. Back in November 2006, Mao Qun'an, spokesman of Ministry of Health, attempted to deflect international criticisms about abuses in organ transplantation in China, "he conceded, though, that improper human organ transplants have taken place in China because of poor government supervision".[9]

## Organ Transplantation Abuses

Organ trade and organ trafficking have been widely reported in the past two years by the Chinese press, although short of bringing up the allegation of organ harvesting from Falun Gong practitioners held in detention. Such malpractice exists primarily because of three reasons: 1) families or individuals of little means are forced to sell organs to survive the rising costs of living; 2) the existence of nationwide networks involving international organ transplantation tourism to China; 3) state-sanctioned organ harvesting from executed prisoners and detained Falun Gong practitioners. Above all, organ transplantation has become a profit-making industry in China, beyond a mere medical procedure, given the ever-increasing domestic and international demand. *Caijing Magazine*, a prestigious Chinese financial journal, published on February 13, 2012, an in-depth investigative report of how an underground organ trade took place in Chenzhou, Hunan Province, involving a young 17-year-old kidney seller, brokers, doctors, the hospital, as well as an organ recipient, a Malaysian in this case.[10] In February 2012, the Supreme People's Procuratorate in Haidian District of Beijing filed a charge against another network of 16 individuals, who have been involved in the organ trade of at least 51 kidneys worth as much as tens of millions of Chinese yuan. The story was reported by the state-run media and has unveiled how such a network managed to get people to sell organs and have hospitals remove their organs, thereby making handsome profit from this organ trade business.[11]

The most notorious abuse in China's organ transplantation, however, comes from the allegations from the international communities, involving organ removal, often live, from Falun Gong practitioners held in detention. Such practice is against their own will and has occurred on a massive scale according to reports by the overseas press, as well as by the well-known independent investigation conducted by David Matas and David Kilgour, whose book *Bloody Harvest – The Killing of Falun Gong for Their Organs* examines the horrific practice with well-documented cases and analysis. Falun Gong is an ancient meditation practice founded on the principles of "Truthfulness, Compassion, Forbearance" with roots embedded in the Buddha School. It was first introduced to the public in 1992 by Mr. Li Hongzhi and was immediately touted by the Chinese authorities for its health benefits and positive moral impact upon society. In 1998, the Communist Party was paranoid, however, when it found out that some 70 to 100 million Chinese people took up this spiritual practice, outnumbering the membership of the Communist Party. On July 20, 1999, former Communist Party leader Jiang Zemin ordered the campaign of persecution against this spiritual group, imprisoning hundreds of thousands of Falun Gong practitioners and demonizing the meditation practice with its state-run propaganda machinery. Jiang Zemin set up a special "610 Office" to carry out the campaign of persecution, whose power is beyond executive and judicial branches, in an effort to eradicate Falun Gong in China. No legal representation, hence, has been allowed to defend Falun Gong detainees who have been subjected to a variety of torture, psychiatric abuses, and even killing. According to Manfred Nowak, the United Nations Special Rapporteur on Torture, two thirds of torture cases in China's labour camps and jails are related to Falun Gong practitioners held in detention.[12] Over three thousand death cases have been documented by Falun Dafa Information Center.[13] All of these have taken place as a result of Jiang Zemin's personal decree to physically destroy the practitioners of Falun Gong. Human rights watchdogs such as Amnesty International, Human Rights Watch, and the country reports annually prepared by U.S. State Department have been documenting the abuses to this day.

There is persuasive evidence supporting the allegation of David Matas and David Kilgour, especially as to why the detained Falun Gong practitioners have been particularly vulnerable as victims of abuses in organ transplantation. First of all, since July 20, 1999, tens of millions of Falun Gong practitioners stepped forward in public, either in front of government office buildings or Tiananmen Square in Beijing, to appeal for their Constitutional right to follow their personal belief. Their public appeals have always been met with violence and arrests. In order to not affect their family members or workplaces, many of these detained Falun Gong practitioners refused to provide their true identities – this would likely account for their later disappearance without the public's awareness, including their family members. These detained Falun Gong practitioners, thus, have become a sizable pool of candidates for organ removal without known identifications and documentations. Secondly, Falun Gong practitioners are known to be in good health because of their exercise regime, which was publicly recognized by Chinese authorities prior to the suppression. Many of the detained Falun Gong practitioners have reportedly been physically examined including with a blood test upon being arrested. This is particularly meaningful in light of Minister Huang's recent remark on March 23, 2012, "Organ transplantation from executed prisoners is not ideal, primarily because the high fungi and bacteria infection rate".[14] Thirdly, given that no legal representation of detained Falun Gong practitioners has been allowed, torture and even killing them are not subject to any penalty, nor do the perpetrators face any legal consequence – such cruelty, in fact, has often been encouraged by the "610 Office" or the authorities in an effort to coerce these spiritual followers to give up their belief as well as to implement the state policy to eradicate Falun Gong. Removal of organs from detained Falun Gong practitioners, torture and killing Falun Gong practitioners, as a matter of fact, do not even constitute any crime in today's China. Over the past 13 years, not a single individual who is involved in imprisoning, torturing and killing practitioners of Falun Gong for organs or other purposes has been brought to trial in the People's Republic of China, in spite of numerous well-documented cases. Fourthly, as demonstrated by a chart of Tianjin Oriental Organ Transplantation Center,[15] the number of organ transplants performed by this particular hospital rose dramatically since mid-1999, perhaps not by chance as it corresponds to the start of China's persecution of Falun Gong, and the number of organ transplants climbed sharply each year, despite the fact that a voluntary organ donation system was unavailable back then and is still not in place to this day. There are at least over 150 state-authorized organ transplantation hospitals in China; yet, human rights groups estimate that there are 5,000 to 8,000 executions taking place per year in China. Yet, between 2003 and 2006, some 15,000 organ transplants were performed each year – where did the uncounted organs come from? While kidney transplantation will, on average, require a waiting period of three years in the U.S. where an active donor system is in place, some Chinese organ transplantation hospitals advertise in several foreign languages that kidney transplantation can be performed within weeks. For instance, Tianjin Oriental Organ Transplantation Center's advertised waiting period is two weeks, while the Organ Transplantation Research Institute of the Second Hospital affiliated with the People's Liberation Army's Second Medical University in Shanghai (otherwise known as Shanghai Long March Hospital) only requires one week's waiting.[16] Many leading organ transplantation experts around the world are increasingly curious: whose organs are they and who have been those so-called "executed prisoners" since mid-1999?

The recent global media coverage of U.S. asylum seeker Wang Lijun, former police chief of Liaoning Province and Chongqing City, has shed light on the likelihood of his own involvement in snatching organs from detained Falun Gong practitioners, amongst other executed prisoners. According to China's online search engine Baidu, Wang Lijun, with no medical training whatsoever, has engaged in a series of organ transplantation experiments while serving as police chief in Jinzhou City, Liaoning, a province known for massive organ harvesting of Falun Gong detainees according to the investigation by David Matas and David Kilgour. In 2006, Wang Lijun was even awarded by the Chinese authorities for his organ transplantation experiments and he confessed at the award ceremony, "Our scientific achievement comes from several thousand samples from the execution sites".[17] The question, moreover, remains: it is unusual for the City of Jinzhou to execute several thousand prisoners within a two-year tenure there; so who were the actual victims killed as the source of organs for Lijun's experiments?

In its recent "2011 Human Rights Report: China (includes Tibet, Hong Kong, and Macau)", the U.S. Department of State reports:

> In response to allegations that the organs of executed prisoners were harvested for transplant purposes, Vice Minister of Health Huang Jiefu in 2009 stated that inmates are not a proper source for human organs and prisoners must give written consent for their organs to be removed. Overseas and domestic media and advocacy groups continued to report instances of organ harvesting, particularly from Falun Gong practitioners and Uighurs.[18]

**Ethical Issues**

Organ transplantation is arguably one of the great breakthroughs in modern medicine, if it is performed in accordance with law and medical ethics – it is a medical procedure that can both save lives and destroy lives. The World Medical Association adopted a statement on human organ donation and transplantation in the year 2000 and revised it again in the year 2006, with specific ethical requirements.[19] World Health Organization has also provided detailed Guiding Principles on Transplantation of Human Cells, Tissues and Organs.[20] China, like other members of World Health Organization as well as of the World Medical Association, is obligated to abide by the ethical standards in addition to its own regulations. It raises serious concerns when there is lack of transparency regarding the source of organs as well as the number of executions taking place each year in China: who are these prisoners and for what crime are they executed? China should allow independent investigators to look into the allegations of massive organ harvesting from Falun Gong practitioners held in detention. It remains China's state policy to systematically persecute and eradicate this spiritual group starting from July 20, 1999, to this very day. Although Chinese authorities have produced some regulations in recent years for organ transplantation, such measures could only serve, at best, as a whitewashing tool to deflect criticisms from the international communities, short of reinforcement and transparency. As stated in the Universal Declaration of Human Rights, "All human beings are born free and equal in dignity and rights. They are endowed with reason and conscience and should act towards one another in a spirit of brotherhood. Everyone has the right to life, liberty and security of person. No one shall be subjected to torture or to cruel inhuman or degrading treatment or punishment".[21] These fundamental human rights, however, have been routinely violated in China under the Communist rule, as documented by the United Nations, Amnesty International and the press, as well as by some China scholars around the world.

1  Medical Encyclopedia: http://www.wiki8.com/qiguanyizhi_40709/

2  "The Book of Filial Piety"

3  "Book of Zhou Rituals"

4  In organ donations, charity begins with body, http://news3.xinhuanet.com/english/2006-11/16/content_5335427.htm

5  China Defends Its Organ Transplant from Executed Prisoners. http://news.bbc.co.uk/chinese/simp/hi/newsid_8240000/newsid_8243600/8243697.stm

6  Health Ministry: Speed up the establishment of post-death organ donor system. http://news.sina.com.cn/c/2012-03-22/214424159133.shtml

7  Ibid

8  Ibid

9  In organ donations, charity begins with body, http://news3.xinhuanet.com/english/2006-11/16/content_5335427.htm

10  Organ Transplant Tourism Network: http://magazine.caijing.com.cn/2012-02-13/111676437.html

11  The Nation's Largest Human Organ Trade is in Court, Involving Tens of Millions. http://www.fjsen.com/h/2012-02/29/content_7922389.htm

12  Manfred Nowak (2006). "Report of the Special Rapporteur on torture and other cruel, inhuman or degrading treatment or punishment: MISSION TO CHINA." United Nations. p. 13.

13  Falun Dafa Information Center: http://faluninfo.net/

14  China Plans to Abandon Harvesting Organs from Executed Prisoners in Five Years: http://cn.wsj.com/gb/20120323/bch152937.asp

15  Source: Tianjin Oriental Organ Transplantation Center Website

16  The Difficulty in Legislating Organ Transplantation. http://www.lifeweek.com.cn/2006-04-17/0005314976.shtml

17  Wang Lijun's Secret Research Center and Confessed to Serve Organ Transplants. http://www.epochtimes.com/gb/12/4/21/n3571316.htm%E7%8E%8B%E7%AB%8B%E5%86%9B%E7%A5%9E%E7%A7%98%E7%A0%94%E7%A9%B6%E4%B8%AD%E5%BF%83-%E5%9D%A6%E6%89%BF%E4%B8%BA%E5%99%A8%E5%AE%98%E7%A7%BB%E6%A4%8D%E4%BE%9B%E4%BD%93?p=all

18  http://www.state.gov/j/drl/rls/hrrpt/2011/eap/186268.htm

19  WMA Statement on Human Organ Donation and Transplantation. http://www.wma.net/en/30publications/10policies/t7/index.html

20  WHO Guiding Principles on Transplantation of Human Cells, Tissues and Organs. http://www.who.int/transplantation/en/index.html

21  Universal Declaration of Human Rights. http://www.un.org/en/documents/udhr/

# Numbers

## DAVID MATAS

How many organ transplants are there each year in China? What are the sources of these organs?

David Kilgour and I, in a report published first in July 2006 and then January 2007,[1] concluded that there were 41,500 transplants in the six year period 2000 to 2005 where the only explanation for the sourcing was Falun Gong practitioners. In November 2009, our book *Bloody Harvest – The Killing of Falun Gong for their Organs* concluded that since our report, matters had gotten worse, that there had been an increase in sourcing of organs from Falun Gong practitioners.[2]

The Government of China acknowledges that organs for transplants done in China come overwhelmingly from Chinese prisoners. The claim of the Government of China is that these prisoners who are the source of organs harvested for transplants are convicted criminals sentenced to death and then executed and before execution, gave consent to the use of their organs for transplants.

In July of 2005, Huang Jiefu, Chinese Deputy Minister of Health, indicated as high as 95% of organs derive from execution.[3] Speaking at a conference of surgeons in the southern city of Guangzhou in mid-November 2006, he said: "Apart from a small portion of traffic victims, most of the organs from cadavers are from executed prisoners".[4] In October 2008, he said "In China, more than 90% of transplanted organs are obtained from executed prisoners".[5] In March 2010, he stated that "... over 90% of grafts from deceased donors are from executed prisoners".[6]

As one can see, at some points, Huang Jiefu refers to deceased donor sources and at other points to all sources. The questions then become, how many live donors are there and how many persons are sentenced to death and then executed? Answering the second question, how many persons are sentenced to death and then executed is not that easy, since the Chinese State and the Communist Party which runs the State consider this information to be a state secret. We are left with external estimates. David Kilgour and I concluded, in our report and book, that the bulk of prisoners who are the source of organs for transplants are Falun Gong practitioners who do not consent, who are killed by the organ harvesting operation and are not sentenced to death.

Falun Gong is a set of exercises with a spiritual foundation first banned by the Communist Party and then the Government of China in 1999 out of jealousy of its popularity and fear that its spirituality, rooted in ancient Chinese traditions, would undermine the ideological supremacy of Western imported Communism. After the banning, Falun Gong practitioners were arrested in the hundreds of thousands. Those who recanted spontaneously or after torture were released.

Those who refused to recant disappeared into what the Government of China euphemistically calls re-education through labour camps. These camps are both arbitrary detention slave labour camps and vast live organ donor banks. The Laogai Research Foundation estimated in 2008 that the number in the camps then currently detained was between 500,000 and two million souls.[7]

David Kilgour and I drew the figure of 41,500 by looking at volumes of transplants and volumes of executions before and after the persecution of Falun Gong began. After the persecution of Falun Gong began, transplant volumes shot up but executions remained steady. So we attributed the difference in transplant sources to Falun Gong. After the release of the second version of our report and before the publication of our book, executions decreased and transplant volumes, after an initial dip, returned to traditional levels. So we concluded that sourcing from Falun Gong practitioners had increased.

What has happened since November 2009 to justify revisiting the numbers issue? There have been developments, though not necessarily ones which give us more information.

Amnesty International has stopped publishing death penalty statistics. It used to provide a death penalty log, setting out individual cases. The last log, published in 2002 set out executions for 2000. Amnesty International continued with yearly estimates after 2002 of persons sentenced to death and then executed, but its last statistics for 2008 of 1,718 executions was published in our book. There are no statistics for 2009 or 2010. The organization gave no explanation for stopping either the log or the statistics.

The loss of information is regrettable. The log and the statistics were based on media reports. While not every execution was publicly reported, thus the log and statistics gave a number lower than total executions, the figures were useful for indicating trends and characteristics. One could see from the log and statistics which Amnesty International compiled the breakdowns, for instance, by crime, region and gender. Amnesty International should re-establish its log and statistical reporting.

For our book, David Kilgour and I were able to garner useful information about transplant volumes from the China Liver Transplant Registry in Hong Kong.[8] In a second development, the China Liver Transplant Registry has now shut down public access to statistical aggregate data on its site. Access is available only to those who have a Registry issued login name and password.

There is some information still publicly accessible, including the names and location of transplant hospitals reporting to the Registry. That listing tells us that military as well as civilian hospitals are reporting. The Registry lists 35 national hospitals including 9 military and 45 provincial hospitals including 11 military.[9]

At The Transplantation Congress in Vancouver in August 2010, Haibo Wang, assistant director of the China Liver Transplant Registry, presented at the same session I did. I asked him why public access to the data on the Registry website was shut down and if it could be restored. His answer was that public access was shut down because people were misinterpreting the data. If anyone is to get access now, the Registry has to know, first, the purpose for which the data is being used and have some confidence that the data will not be misinterpreted.

The Chinese health system runs four transplant registries, one each for liver, kidney, heart and lung. The other three are located in mainland China – kidney[10] and heart[11] in Beijing and lung[12] in Wuxi. The data on the other three sites is also accessible only to those who have Registry issued login names and passwords.

When China took over Hong Kong from Britain, the unification was based on the principle of one country, two systems. However, when it comes to public access to aggregate statistical transplant data, there is now one country with one system.

The World Health Organization Guiding Principle 11 requires transparency of sources, open to scrutiny, while ensuring that personal anonymity of donors and recipients are protected. Hiding aggregate data from the public which were previously available directly contradicts this principle. Aggregate data from all four transplant registries should be publicly accessible without the need for a login name and password.

Though these developments since *Bloody Harvest* do not justify re-examination of our numerical conclusions, they do deserve comment. Murder of innocents is harder in broad daylight. The darkness cast by data cover-up makes organ transplant abuse easier to perpetrate. One factor which drove our conclusion that Falun Gong were being killed for their organs is that the mechanisms which should be in place to prevent such an abuse were not in place. That conclusion is even truer now than when we published our book because data publicly available then through the China Liver Transplant Registry which indicated the extent of the abuse is no longer available.

A third development since *Bloody Harvest* was published is the establishment of an organ donation system. The Chinese Ministry of Health, under the supervision of the Chinese Red Cross, in March 2010 set up an organ donation system in 11 provinces and municipalities. This system is limited to donation after cardiac death. It does not contemplate either living donations or donations after brain death only.

The newspaper *Beijing Today* reported in March 2011, one year later, "In Nanjing, the capital of Jiangsu Province, (one of the eleven sites), not one person has elected to be a donor". Liu Wenhua, a member of the Red Cross of Nanjin and one of 12 donation counsellors sent by the city government to five hospitals said "only three people in Nanjing have donated organs in the past 20 years". The story goes on to note: "Success was equally absent in other regions. As of last Thursday, only 37 people nationwide had registered to donate their organs".[13] There is no indication how many, if any, of these 37 had died during the year, resulting in actual donations.

These donations, if any, are statistically insignificant and can not change our conclusions. Nonetheless, the failed effort is worth noting. The very failure indicates the lack of seriousness of the Communist Party/Chinese State combat in overcoming the cultural aversion to donations. For the Party/State, changing organ sourcing from prisoners is not a priority.

A fourth development is a statistical snapshot we glimpsed in March 2010 when Chinese Deputy Health Minister Huang Jiefu gave a speech to a transplant conference in Madrid. At that conference, he selectively released the information hidden in the four transplant registries. The historical information is consistent with what was known before. The new information brings the data up to date to the time of his speech, admittedly only a few months after our book was published.

The speech, though, is not completely reliable because it is internally inconsistent. Huang Jiefu produces, in a slide show presentation, one slide showing the number of kidney and liver transplants in China over the past decade. He produces a second slide showing living donor vs. deceased donor kidney transplantation from 2003 to 2009. The second slide produces totals for living and deceased donations (non-heart beating donations - NHBD). So there are two slides which have kidney transplant totals for the period 2003 to 2009. These two slides have conflicting information.

The first slide shows kidney transplants for 2009 to be 6,458. The second shows the figure as 6,485. There is presumably a transposition error here. However, because we cannot check the original figures, we do not know which is correct.

For 2008, the figure for both slides is 6,274. This is useful information because it shows we are not considering two different types of data.

For 2007, the figure for the first slide is 7,700 and for the second slide is 3,974. This is a significant difference, without explanation.

For 2006, the difference is also large, 8,000 for the first slide, 3,021 for the second slide. Similarly for 2005, we have 8,500 for the first slide and 3,441 for the second. For 2004, we have an astonishing figure of 10,000 for the first slide and 3,461 for the second. For 2003, we have 5,500 for the first slide and 3,171 for the second.

Because for 2007 and earlier years on the first slide we have rounded numbers, and for the second slide precise numbers, it appears that, for the earlier years on the second slide, we are not looking at totals but rather a subset. The first slide, it seems, presents estimates. The second set presents, it would seem, the subtotal of reported kidney transplants which provide the necessary differentiated information to allow the construction of the second table.

The second Huang Jiefu table differentiates between living and deceased donor kidney transplants. Kidney transplant information which does not distinguish between living and deceased sources would be useless for the construction of this table. So, presumably, it was just pushed aside.

Huang Jiefu, mind you, says none of this. He just blithely presents contradictory information without explanation and hides the data sets from the public on which he based his tables.

If the analysis here is correct, then the larger totals of the first table are the better ones. The larger, though, the totals, the more that is needed to explain the sources. Where in the world did 10,000 kidneys and 2,265 livers come from in 2004? It was not from living donors.

Another table Huang Jiefu presents is living vs. deceased donor liver transplantation. That table shows significant living donor sources starting from 2007. Living donors are 23.5% of liver transplants in 2007, 19.1% in 2008 and 13.6% in 2009. However, for 2004, living donors are a mere .4% of total donations.

Huang Jiefu does not give comparable figures for kidney transplants. I suspect that the reason is that the figures would look nowhere near as good. The volume of kidney transplants has been, in recent years, three times or more the volume of liver transplants.

The most likely hypothesis is that kidney transplant living donors are the same absolute number in any year as the liver transplant living donors. That would mean that the percentage of kidney transplant living donors would be, in percentage terms, one third or less of the percentage of liver transplant living donors.

Living donations, according to the Huang Jiefu text, are given to "related or kinship recipients". This is hardly surprising given the parlous state of the donor system in China. Persuading a relative to donate to a family member who needs an organ is one technique for overcoming the cultural aversion to donation, a technique which appears to have met in China with significant success. It is an indicator that other techniques, if tried with any real effort, would also work.

Huang Jiefu talks, in his speech, about how organ transplantation was initially an unregulated business. He does not say this, but the overall impression he leaves is that any hospital which wanted got into the business of transplants and sold transplants to whomever they wanted, getting organs from whatever source on which they could lay their hands. It is apparent that this sort of system would not produce reliable statistics, that any information about volumes would just be estimates.

A law which took effect on May 1, 2007, required that transplants take place only in registered hospitals.[14] The law set up a registration system for hospitals. The statistics we see for 2008 and 2009 come, presumably, from the registered hospitals which is why we get precise figures in both slides for those years. From 2009, estimates from a hospital free for all became unnecessary.

A fifth development is changes to the death penalty. Vice President Zhang Jun of the Supreme People's Court, in January 2011, stated that China's Supreme People's Court would overturn death sentences in cases where evidence was collected by illegal means.

The judge said that the move was intended to limit the application of capital punishment and pressure local courts to check evidence more thoroughly.[15]

The China National People's Congress Standing Committee amended the Criminal Law in February 2011 to decrease the number of death penalty offences from 68 to 55. In a second change, the death penalty could no longer be imposed on those 75 years or older at the time of trial, except for a person who had committed a murder with "exceptional cruelty".[16] The new law came into effect May 1.

The Supreme People's Court (SPC) wrote, in its annual report released in May 2011, that the death penalty should only be applied to "a very small number" of criminals who have committed "extremely serious crimes". Chinese courts were told to pronounce a two-year suspension of execution for condemned criminals if an immediate execution was not deemed necessary; capital punishment reprieves could be granted as long as they were allowed by law.

This downward slide in the death penalty continues a previous trend. The most significant prior development was the requirement, which took effect on January 1, 2007, that all death sentences had to be approved by the Supreme People's Court. That change alone led to a reduction of an estimated 30% to 40% in the imposition of the death penalty.

In the abstract, from a human rights perspective, the reduction in the death penalty is good news. The news ceases though to be good if the decrease in the death penalty leads to an increase in the killing of Falun Gong for their organs. While the decrease in the death penalty has occurred at the same time as the increase of living donor transplants, the increase in living donor transplants has come nowhere near the estimated decrease in the death penalty.

A sixth development since the publication of *Bloody Harvest* has been the work of Ethan Gutmann and Jaya Gibson. Their work, first announced in June 2010[17] and elaborated on in another chapter in this book, tells us that the killing of innocents for their organs has spread from Falun Gong to Tibetans, Eastern Lightning House Christians and Uighurs. They glean this information from interviewing members of these victim groups who got out of Chinese detention centres and then out of China. Those interviewed tell them of blood testing and organ examination of the sort that Falun Gong practitioners endured.

This phenomenon means we cannot ascribe the difference between transplant volumes and death penalty volumes to Falun Gong practitioners alone. Some of the sources will be these other victim groups.

A seventh development is the bizarre publication in the *Journal of the American Medical Association* in July 2011 of some Communist Party propaganda about organ transplants in China, a commentary title "Regulation of Organ Transplantation in China: Difficult Exploration and Slow Advance" by Shi Bing-Yi and Chen Li-Ping, members of the Chinese military, the People's Liberation Army.[18] This publication violates medical ethics.

The Transplantation Society Ethics Committee Policy Statement on the Chinese Transplantation Program states: "presentations of studies involving patient data or samples from recipients of organs or tissues from executed prisoners should not be accepted". The editors and associate editors of the journal *Liver Transplantation* wrote that they "have decided that original publications dealing with clinical liver transplantation outcomes submitted to this journal should explicitly exclude the use of executed prisoners or paid donors as a source of donor organs".[19] Publication of the Commentary violated the spirit of these standards.

What is more, Shi Bing-Yi, one of the co-authors, has a history of stating what the Communist Party wants him to say about organ harvesting even though it contradicts his own previous statements. Dr. Shi Bing-Yi said in an article posted on *Health Paper Net* in March 2006 that there were about 90,000[20] transplants in total up until 2005. The text stated, in part, in translation:

> Professor Shi Bing-Yi said that in the past 10 years, organ transplantation in China had grown rapidly; the types of transplant operations that can be performed were very wide, ranging from kidney, liver, heart, pancreas, lung, bone marrow, cornea; so far, there had been over 90,000 transplants completed country-wide; last year alone, there was close to 10,000 kidney transplants and nearly 4,000 liver transplants completed.

David Kilgour and I referred to this total and this article in our report, *Bloody Harvest*. Manfred Nowak, the United Nations Rapporteur on Torture, asked the Government of China to explain the discrepancy between volume of organ transplants and volume of identified sources, relying, in part, on our report and its reference to the Shi Bing-Yi article. The Chinese government, in a response sent to the Rapporteurs by letter dated March 19, 2007, and published in the report of Professor Nowak to the UN Human Rights Council dated February 19, 2008, stated that:

> Professor Shi Bing-Yi expressly clarified that on no occasion had he made such a statement or given figures of this kind, and these allegations and the related figures are pure fabrication.

Shi Bing-Yi was interviewed in a video documentary produced by Phoenix TV, a Hong Kong media outlet. That video shows Shi

Bing-Yi on screen saying what the Government of China, in its response to Nowak, indicates he said that the figures we quote from him he simply never gave. He is wearing a military uniform, perhaps to indicate that we should not take too seriously what he is saying, that he is only following orders. He says on the video:

> I did not make such a statement because I have no knowledge of these figures. I have not made detailed investigation on this subject how many were carried out and in which year. Therefore I have no figures to show. So I could not have said that.

Yet, the actual source, the *Health News Network* article, in June 2008, remained on its original Chinese website, though it has been taken down since. The original source of the information remained available within China through the internet at the time Shi Bing-Yi denied the information.

So we have to approach the Commentary published by the *Journal of the American Medical Association* both with repugnance and a grain of salt. It does have, nonetheless, some data consistent with other data.

The Commentary observes that with the (after cardiac death) donation system set up as a pilot project in eleven cities "more than 200 individuals" volunteered to donate their organs and that "only 63 were able to do so by the end of May 2011". To say, as the authors do, that only 63 "were able" to die in a certain period is, to say the least, an odd way of putting things. One has, I think, to be a dyed in the wool member of the Communist Party of China to characterize staying alive as an inability. Yet, the Commentary does confirm the point that this donation system is statistically insignificant as a source for organs.

Where does this leave us? Our figure of 41,500 was generated by comparing transplant volumes before and after the persecution of Falun Gong began. The most reliable death penalty statistics came from Amnesty International. Though they were almost certainly an underestimate because based on media reports alone, we considered them reliable indicators of multi-year trends, if not yearly totals. Multi-year averages of executions, according to Amnesty International figures, remained constant before and after the persecution of Falun Gong. The difference between transplant volumes before and after the persecution of Falun Gong could then reasonably be attributed to Falun Gong sourcing.

Another methodological approach, used by researcher H. Li, is to take the highest estimate of death penalty execution volumes and work from there.[21] The high estimate to which he refers is 10,000 yearly, published in 2004. This 2004 yearly estimate of 10,000 came from Chen Zhonglin, a National People's Congress delegate who, with others, was urging a review of all death sentences by the Supreme People's Court,[22] a reform which eventually happened in 2007.

Chen made clear that his estimate was not an official figure and was based on tabulations.[23] In other words, he was guessing in a context where a high figure helped to support the reform he advocated. In any case, even if we take Chen's estimate at face value, it reduces to 7,000 by the time the reforms he advocated were implemented, since they generated at least a 30% reduction in volume of executions.

Since we do not know with precision the number of executions, another tack is trying to figure out the volume of executions which would support the volume of transplants, a figure which we have. The volume of executions has to be a multiple of the number of transplants for a variety of reasons.

One reason is the absence of a national organ distribution system. Individual hospitals make arrangements with individual prisons for organs. There is substantial organ wastage in China.

A second reason is that transplanting several organs at once from the same donor contradicts the recipient information. Everywhere else patients wait for donors. In China, sources wait for patients. Once the patients are ready, the sources are killed.

Given the short waiting times for transplants and the absence of a national organ distribution system, sourcing several organs from the same donor would require recipient coordination. Yet, our interviews with recipients show no such coordination.

A third reason relates to the Chinese government claim that donors consent. While there is no proof of this consent, let us take the Chinese government claim at face value, that persons sentenced to death actually do consent. Then consider the failure of the national donor system in operation for now over a year.

As noted, a newspaper report shows 37 consents in a year throughout 11 cities. *The Journal of the American Medical Association* Commentary shows around 200 consents until May 2011. This low rate of consent is attributed to cultural aversion to donations. Yet prisoners sentenced to death in China come from the same culture as other Chinese and would have the same cultural aversion to donation. There is no reason to believe that their consent, if freely given, would occur at any different rate than consents outside of prison.

So we are left with a choice. Either the consents of persons in prison sentenced to death, like the consents of persons outside of prison, are statistically insignificant. Or the notion of prisoner consent is just a sham, one more piece of Communist propaganda.

The prison environment and impending execution may induce consents which would otherwise not be forthcoming. However, consents at a higher rate than the non-prison population because of these factors are indicators of the coercive impact of prison on voluntariness and not indicators of true consent.

As well, though the prison coercive environment may induce rates of nominal consent higher than that of the general population, it is implausible to suggest that the rate of nominal consent would be near or close to 100%, given the almost total reluctance of the non-prison population to consent. Even within a prison atmosphere, there will be, in light of Chinese cultural aversion to donation, a significant proportion of prisoners who will not even nominally consent.

A fourth reason the volume of executions has to be a multiple of the number of transplants is the Criminal Procedure Code of China requirement that a convict sentenced to death be executed seven days after sentence.[24] The Code allows the sentenced to be executed by either injection or shooting.

The interviews David Kilgour and I have had with patients tell us that, if the source of the organ was a prisoner sentenced to death and then executed, the seven day rule was not being respected. For, if it were, then patients would have had, at most, seven days notice of the availability of a transplant and would have been told that the organ would have been available at a precise date.

However, patients were not being told that. They were told, and hospitals were advertising this on their websites, that organs would be available at any time, at the convenience of the patients.

It would be reasonable to assume that the seven day rule for execution was often, even if not universally, applied. That would mean that many prisoners sentenced to death and then executed were not sources of organs for transplants.

Even in a country like China, where there is no rule of law, no independent judiciary, no free media, no democracy, where human rights defenders are repressed, there is some scope for the presumption of legality. Corruption undermines the presumption, but does not replace it altogether.

For prisoners sentenced to death, the corrupt would be tempted to ignore the seven day rule if there was money to be made from transplants. However, it is reasonable to assume that at least some Chinese officials are not corrupt.

The fifth reason the volume of executions has to be a multiple of the number of transplants is the form of execution. Until 2006, the majority of death penalty prisoners were executed by shooting. In a 2006 article for USA Today[25], Liu Renwen, death penalty researcher at the Chinese Academy of Social Sciences, is quoted as saying that the "majority (of executions) are still by gunshot. ... But the use of injections has grown in recent years, and may have reached 40%".

Until January 2008, execution by shooting was common. That month, Jiang Xingchang, the vice president of the Supreme People's Court, announced to the China Daily an expansion of lethal injections to replace shootings.[26]

Once a person is shot and killed, there is almost immediate organ deterioration. Organ transplants can be sourced from those shot and killed, if the sourcing is done immediately. Injection offers the luxury of time. The bulk of the anecdotal evidence we have, except for the period when China began transplants, is that organ sources are injected and not shot. Many of those executed by shooting, because of the practical reality of immediate organ deterioration and the inability to organize on the spot harvesting, are not organ sources.

A sixth reason is the need for blood type and ideally tissue type compatibility between the donor and the recipient. Not every donor is available as a source for every patient. There are four blood types in the ABO system – A, B, AB and O. There are two blood types in the RH system, Rh+ and Rh-. The ABO blood type distribution in China is A 27%, B 26%, AB 12% and O 35%.[27] The blood type distribution for the Rh factor in China is 99.67% Rh+, .33% Rh-.

For local recipients, the patient blood type distribution would match the prisoner blood type distribution. For transplant tourists, the blood type distribution would depend on the source of tourism.

However, for each recipient, one would need a group of prisoners for a statistical likelihood of a match, more than 1,200 if the recipient has blood type AB Rh negative. Moreover, since sourcing is local, each detention centre with ties to a local hospital has to have its own group of prisoners waiting for execution, its own organ donor bank. The notion that at any one time at all major prisons in China there are hundreds of prisoners sentenced to death and awaiting execution runs contrary to observed experience.

Then UN Rapporteur on Torture, Manfred Nowak, on his visit to China in November 2005, found in prisons persons sentenced to death, at first instance, awaiting appeal but none sentenced to death awaiting execution.[28] When he asked to see such prisoners, he was told that there were none because all prisoners sentenced to death whose appeals had been exhausted were executed immediately.

A seventh reason the volume of executions has to be a multiple of the number of transplants is blood disease which renders transplantation unsuitable. The most common such blood disease is hepatitis B, which is endemic in China. One study estimated 50% to 60% of the Chinese population carries hepatitis B markers.[29] Another study focused on four Chinese cities found the infection rate to be 62.6%.[30]

If we look just at this last reason alone, we would need 267 prisoners for every 100 organ recipients. If we put the other factors into the mix, we are looking at more like a factor of ten to one. That is to say, 10,000 organ transplants a year, if the sourcing is solely prisoners sentenced to death and then executed, would require something in the order of 100,000 executions a year.

One has, of course, to take into account the increased sourcing from living organ donors. On the other side of the ledger are the death penalty developments which have cut down substantially on executions.

The bottom line is that the volume of prisoners sentenced to death and then executed necessary to sustain the current rate of transplantation is so out of whack with every death penalty estimate in China, by far, as well as Chinese death penalty execution procedures that organ sourcing, preponderantly, must be coming from other sources than prisoners sentenced to death and then executed. And what would those other sources be?

Tibetans, Uighurs and Eastern Lightning House Christians, sources Ethan Gutmann and Jaya Gibson have identified, are unlikely to come anywhere near the necessary volume. Uighurs and Tibetans are detained in specific geographical locations in China, not throughout China. Eastern Lightning House Christians suffer nowhere near the rate of detention or extremes of vilification of Falun Gong. Falun Gong practitioner prisoners remain the most plausible source for the bulk of transplants in China.

Numbers in this context are just guesswork. My guess, for what it is worth, is that the source of the 10,000 transplants a year in China is 1,000 from prisoners sentenced to death and then executed, 500 from living donor relatives, 500 from Tibetans, Uighurs and Eastern Lightning House Christians and 8,000 from Falun Gong practitioners.

Be that as it may, the onus does not lie on me to prove these numbers. The onus lies rather on the Government of China to provide the numbers. The current situation creates a presumption of wrongdoing beyond the sourcing of organs from prisoners sentenced to death and then executed.

Organ transplant sourcing must be transparent and traceable. The Government of China admits that organs are sourced predominantly from prisoners. What then is it trying to hide by not providing numbers? One compelling answer is that it is trying to hide the  killing of Falun Gong and other prisoners of conscience for their organs.

The claim that the sources have consented, as unpersuasive as it is for prisoners sentenced to death, would be impossible for innocent sources. The killing of innocents for their organs is murder. The killing of prisoners of conscience for their organs is a crime against humanity.

Criminals against humanity typically make every effort to cover-up their crimes. The secrecy we see about numbers looks to be just that – a cover-up of a crime against humanity.

1 At www.organharvestinvestigation.net

2 Chapter eight.

3 The Congressional Executive Commission on China Annual Report 2006, p. 59, note 224, p.201: "Organ Transplants: A Zone of Accelerated Regulation" *Caijing Magazine* (Online), 28 November 05.

4 http://news3.xinhuanet.com/english/2006-11/16/content_5335427.htm

5 http://press.thelancet.com/chinaorgan.pdf

6 "Tomorrow's Organ Transplantation Program in China", Presentation delivered at the Madrid Conference on Organ Donation and Transplantation, Madrid 2010, by Prof. Huang Jiefu, Vice Minister of Health, P.R.C.

7 Laogai Handbook 2007-2008 page 18 at http://laogai.org/system/files/u1/handbook2008-all.pdf

8 Liver Transplant Registry, www.cltr.org, Queen Mary Hospital, The University of Hong Kong, Hong Kong

9 https://www.cltr.org/en/transplantcenters.jsp

10 Kidney Transplant Registry, www.csrkt.org

11 PLA No. 309 Hospital, Beijing, Heart Transplant Registry, www.cotr.cn, effective from April 2010, Fuwai Cardiovascular Hospital, Chinese Academy of Medical Sciences, Beijing

12 Lung Transplant Registry, www.cotr.cn, effective from April 2010, Wuxi People's Hospital, Wuxi

13 Han Manman "Organ donor pilot a failure after one year," March 18, 2011 http://www.beijingtoday.com.cn/feature/organ-donor-pilot-a-failure-after-one-year

14 Regulations on Human Organ Transplant

15 People's Daily, 10/01/2011

16 China at www.handsoffcain.info.

17 Ethan Gutmann, "China's Policies Toward Spiritual Movements" Congressional-Executive Commission on China, Roundtable discussion, Friday, June 18, 2010; Julia Duin, "China accused of vast trade in organs," *Washington Times*, April 27, 2010

18 Issue of July 27, 2011, Vol 306, No. 4.

19  Issue 13:182, 2007

20  http://www.transplantation.org.cn/html/2006-03/394.html (Health
    Paper Net 2006-03-02) Archived page:
    http://archive.edoors.com/render.php?uri=http%3A%2F%2Fwww.
    transplantation.org.cn%2Fhtml%2F200603%2F394.
    html+&x=32&y=11

21  Forced Organ Harvesting in China

22  "China executes 10,000 people a year - NPC delegate" AFP
    March 15, 2004.

23  Amnesty International "Executed, according to law? - The death
    penalty in China"

24  In Article 211.

25  Calum MacLeod "China makes ultimate punishment mobile"
    6/14/2006

26  Xie Chuanjiao, "Lethal injection to be used more", 2008-01-03, http://
    www.chinadaily.com.cn/cndy/2008-01/03/content_6366317.htm

27  http://answers.yahoo.com/question/
    index?qid=20081004023622AAepoS

28  Report of the Special Rapporteur on torture and other cruel,
    inhuman or degrading treatment or punishment, Manfred Nowak,
    Mission to China, UN Document number E/CN.4/2006/6/Add.6,
    10 March 2006

29  "Prevalence of Serological Hepatitis B Markers in a Working
    Population in Hefei, China" *Asia Pacific Journal of Public Health*
    vol. 1 no. 4 (October 1987): 28-33

30  "Hepatitis B Virus Prevalence in Industrialized Cities in China"
    *Asia Pacific Journal of Public Health* vol. 5 no. 4 (October 1991):
    350-358

# Persecution of Falun Gong

## DAVID KILGOUR and JAN HARVEY

China's 5000+ year old civilization has given much to the world and is richly deserving of respect internationally. The Chinese people at home and in many diasporas abroad have excelled in virtually every field of endeavour. In this chapter, however, the focus is on Chinese Communist Party (CCP) practices imported from European Leninism and the party-state governance model in place since seizing power in 1949. The systematic abuse of targeted individuals and groups deemed "enemies" of the party has in its most extreme form resulted in widespread pillaging of vital organs from Falun Gong practitioners for commercial transplantation purposes.

The Party has unleashed a series of campaigns intended to enhance or preserve its monopoly on political control. Since the 1950s, not a decade has gone by without party-state-led violence directed at segments of the population, who were normally labeled "counter-revolutionaries". This includes Mao Zedong's "Great Leap Forward," which resulted in the death by starvation of 25 to 40 million Chinese from 1959 to 1961, the Cultural Revolution, the 1989 crackdown on the democracy movement, and most recently the persecution of Falun Gong since mid-1999.

### From Encouragement to Persecution

When Falun Gong exercises and principles were initially introduced to the Chinese public in 1992, the party-state in Beijing not only acquiesced to its expansion, but even assisted the movement, inviting its founder to teach in government facilities and praising it for the benefits it introduced to public health and ethics generally.

The more the movement grew, however, the more resistance it encountered because some Party leaders feared any large, independent group.

When Falun Gong books became bestsellers in 1996, they were banned.

When a government survey estimated that more than 70 million people were practitioners in the mid-1990s, more than the Party's then membership, state media began attacking the movement and security began to spy on and harass adherents.

An article in the February 14, 1999, issue of *U.S. News & World Report* cited an official in the Sports Ministry saying that each Falun Gong practitioner was saving the state 1,000 yuan in health spending yearly.[1] However, Party leader Jiang Zemin made an overnight decision to eradicate it, even though at the time many members of the Politburo were familiar with the practice and many Party members were doing the exercises.

On July 22, 1999, the Falun Gong movement was officially banned by the Party, thus commencing a protracted, violent campaign of persecution.

## 610 Office

The 610 Office, an agency specifically created to persecute Falun Gong adherents, was given absolute power over each level of the party-state administration, including all political and judicial offices, all media, the army and police. Security personnel began to arrest and detain practitioners across the country.[2]

Beatings, detention in forced labour camps, brainwashing and torture became the daily lot of many practitioners. The torture methods included hanging victims from ceilings, shocking them with high-voltage electric batons, sleep deprivation, starvation, sexual assault, forced abortions, drug injections and brutal force-feeding.

Most of the abuse took place in secret behind closed doors, in detention centres, labour camps, and mountainside torture chambers. As totalitarian regimes engaged in systematic human rights violations frequently do, the Party went to great lengths to hide what it was doing from journalists, scholars, human rights organizations and other independent researchers.

Chinese citizens who tried to investigate the abuses risked losing their careers, freedom and their lives. Foreign journalists in China could lose their work permits. Falun Gong adherents who acted as informants to foreign media were detained or imprisoned, tortured or worse.

In October 1999, Party leaders arbitrarily labeled the movement "an evil cult" to justify its ban retroactively.

Journalists and insiders described then Party leader and President Jiang Zemin as "jealous" of the group and "obsessed" with eradicating it. By creating a national campaign, he sought to consolidate political power to himself and eliminate a movement he perceived as a threat to his power.

Falun Gong is a practice of self-cultivation and its practitioners have no desire to become involved in political affairs. The CCP perceived it, with its principles of truthfulness, compassion and tolerance, as a threat to the communist system, which governs, to a large extent, through corruption. Richard McGregor's 2010 book, *The Party*, notes that since 1982 "about 80 per cent of the 130,000 to 190,000 officials disciplined annually for malfeasance by the Party received only a warning. Only 6 per cent were criminally prosecuted, and of them, only 1 per cent went to jail".[3]

## Representative Falun Gong Victims

According to the testimonies of many witnesses and family members of Falun Gong, many of the practitioners persecuted to death and whose bodies had been returned to their families had their organs stolen. Normally, families only received ashes after loved ones had been cremated without family consent. Testimony also came from practitioners, who had been held in prisons or other camps and who were eventually released or escaped, that they were forced to undergo all kinds of physical health exams and blood tests. This always puzzled them because, since they had been treated so inhumanly, they could not understand why the authorities wanted to know or cared about their state of health.

## Chen Qi Dong

"L", a former prisoner from China interviewed in July 2008 by David Matas, recounted that, while imprisoned, he was kept in various prison cells averaging twenty persons per cell. In over ten instances, one of his cell mates was a prisoner sentenced to death. "L" became familiar with the barbaric execution practices.

A few days before an execution, a man in a white coat would come and extract a blood sample from the condemned individual. On the execution day, four or five men in white coats with white gloves would arrive. They would escort the man outside to a waiting white ambulance van displaying a red cross. All this was visible through the prison windows.

In one case, when "L" was under interrogation, he saw one of the death penalty inmates in an adjoining room with a needle and syringe sticking out of his neck. The syringe was half full of liquid. An hour later the prisoner was still there, but the syringe was empty. When "L" returned from interrogation, his cell leader told him that the prisoner was being injected with an anesthetic to make him numb and preserve his organs until they could be seized.

In this manner, "L" learned from cell leaders that prisoners sentenced to death were being organ pillaged for transplants. Their dates for execution were set with a nearby hospital and arranged for the precise times when organs were needed for transplantation. The money paid for the organs was split fifty-fifty between the hospital and the prison guards.

In November 2006, "L" was transferred to cell 311 in #1 prison, Wu Xi City, near Shanghai from another cell. Shortly after his arrival, guards asked him to sign a statement that prisoner Chen Qi Dong had died of illness. The guards wanted it to show to Chen's family. Chen Qi Dong had been in cell 311, but died a few days before "L" was transferred to the same cell. "L" had never met him and refused to sign the statement about his cause of death. Others in the cell signed.

The cell 311 leader and eight other cell members told "L" what happened. Because Chen was a Falun Gong practitioner who refused to recant and insisted on continuing exercises while in prison, guards had beaten and tortured him. In response, Chen began a hunger strike. The guards force fed him by pouring congee, rice porridge, down a tube jammed into his throat. The congee was too hot and scalded his digestive system, causing him to contract a fever.

At this point, a man in white arrived and took a blood sample a few days before Chen was taken from his cell. The day he left for the final time, four men with white coats and white gloves came to remove him. One of the prisoners in the cell, that day in interrogation, saw Chen in the next room, with a needle in his neck. Through a window, the prisoners in cell 311 could see a white hospital ambulance van with a red cross waiting. The cell leader told "L" that Chen had been organ harvested.

During his stay in prison, "L" learned of two or three other such cases, but without the details available in the Chen case. There was, however, a similar pattern. Practitioners refused to recant and continued their meditation and exercises in prison. The guards beat and tortured them in response, to a point where the practitioner was permanently injured. The guards, in order to remove evidence of their crimes, arranged for any physical evidence to disappear through organ pillaging from the practitioners.

For the full statement of "L" see the web site which hosts the Matas/Kilgour report: http://organharvestinvestigation.net/events/D_Matas_081408.htm.

### Chen Ying

Chen Ying, a Falun Gong refugee accepted by France:

> Because I would not renounce my Falun Gong convictions, between Feb 2000 and Nov 2001, I was imprisoned three times without any judicial process. ... Each time, I was mistreated and tortured by the police. ... At the end of September, 2000 ... I was called out by the police and taken to a hospital for a complete medical examination: cardiac, blood, eyes, etc. ... The police injected me with unknown substances. After the injections, my heart beat abnormally quickly. Each one gave me the impression that my heart was going to explode. ...[4]

### Wang Bin

Wang was arrested after appealing to the government in Beijing for the right to practice Falun Gong. Taken to the Dongfeng Xinchun

Labour Camp in Daqing City, he was tortured extensively and died in detention from his injuries on October 4, 2000. After his death, his heart was removed without the consent of his family.[5]

## Yang Ruiyu

Yang Ruiyu was a practitioner from Fuzhou City, Fujian Province. An employee of the Housing Management Bureau of the Taijiang District, she was taken away from work on July 19, 2001. Three days later, she died as a result of abuse. After her death, the police threatened her family not to leak any information. Her colleagues were not allowed to see her body, and no funeral was permitted. When her body was sent to be cremated, it was guarded by police cars and cremated immediately upon arrival. Yang's husband and daughter were not allowed to see the body.

## Yang Zhongfang

Thirty-seven-year-old Yang was a Falun Gong practitioner from Chengdu City in Sichuan Province. At 6:00 a.m. on July 1, 2002, Jiangong police surrounded her home and arrested Yang, her husband, son and daughter. That night, Ms. Yang was beaten to death in custody. When her relatives arrived at the police station, they learned that her internal organs had been removed and that her body had been sent to a crematorium. Officials claimed that she had died from "more than a dozen acute illnesses". In fact, Yang was healthy, as indicated in her annual physical examinations.[6]

### Timeline on Organ Pillaging Across China

1984:  After the introduction of cyclosporine, China implemented a rule to allow for organ donation from executed prisoners. The "Rules Concerning the Utilization of Corpses or Organs for the Corpses of Executed Prisoners" provided "that corpses or organs of executed prisoners could be harvested if no one claimed the body, if the executed prisoner volunteered to have his corpse so used, or if the family consented".[7]

What constituted a crime punishable by death? An Amnesty International researcher found that criminals were executed for minimal offences, such as pig stealing or theft. Amnesty International later asserted that the Chinese government was performing executions to expand the organ trade from executed prisoners. According to witnesses in China, criminals were regularly examined to select matches for waiting patients. "One prisoner, during his seven year jail term, told how he saw numerous prisoners being medically prepared for organ removal. On the night before the execution, the prison staff would take blood samples".[8]

1990s: China executed more people than the rest of the world combined.[9] Human rights organizations were outraged by the alleged human organ donation from China's executed prisoners.

2000: China stood alone in continuing the use of organs of executed prisoners for transplant surgery.[10]

2005: The Director of the Transplant Center of the People's Liberation Army said that in 2005 alone, there were approximately 10,000 kidney transplants and 4,000 liver transplants. (In 1999, there were only 4,000 kidney transplants and no liver transplants.)[11]

Deputy Health Minister Huang Jiefu was reported to have said that as many as 95% of the transplanted organs in China derived from executions. The transplant volume went up dramatically after the banning of Falun Gong, yet there were no signs that the number of persons sentenced to death and then executed did actually increase.

2006: The number of transplants reached a record of 20,000 transplants.[12]

*March 9:* A Chinese investigative journalist reported that at a provincial hospital in Northeast China, doctors were harvesting organs from Falun Gong detainees for profit. About 6,000 practitioners were in a concentration camp in Sujiatun, Shen Yang City, Liaoning Province. There was a crematory and no practitioner had come out alive.

Before the Sujiatun situation was revealed, a number of witnesses had stated that the bodies of many practitioners who had been tortured to death had had their organs stolen.[13]

*March 17:* "Annie", another witness, a former staff member at the Sujiatun Hospital and ex-wife of a former corneal surgeon who had been involved in the live organ harvesting activity at the hospital, affirmed the journalist's allegations. She revealed that after practitioners' bodies were pillaged of their livers, kidneys, corneas and other organs, the bodies were immediately cremated to destroy the evidence. By disclosing this crime, she hoped to save lives and also to help redeem her ex-husband. She also stated that the Sujiatun Labour Camp had begun its inhuman organ pillaging for profit as early as 2001 and reached its peak in 2003.

By 2006, organ transplants had increased dramatically. The waiting time for kidneys was only days, while hearts and livers required only a few weeks. The sharp rise in the number of organ transplants and the short waiting time to find a matching donor indicated the presence of a large live organ bank. The recorded number of organ transplants far exceeded the sum total of voluntary organ donation and all death penalty prisoners in China each year. The very large numbers of Falun Gong, considered the number one enemy of the Party, were most likely the source of this unaccounted for organ supply. Some medical staff contacted by phone admitted that organs had come from live Falun Gong. There was a large network in place and everyone got paid: police, detention centres, courts and doctors.[14]

**March 27:** The CCP announced new "Temporal Regulations on Clinical Use and Management of Human Organ Transplants" to take effect on July 1.

The new law required written consent from the organ source, but there was no means of determining whether that consent was obtained. The law also required medical institutions to charge patients according to ministry standards, but this provision was being violated by the exorbitant fees charged to foreigners.

**March 28:** The regime issued a statement denying the existence of the Sujiatun Camp and inviting members of the international community to take a tour through the Thrombosis Hospital at Sujiatun.

**March 31:** A third witness, who identified himself as a veteran military doctor but otherwise remained anonymous, confirmed the practices at Sujiatun, and said that it was just one of 36 similar camps across China. He said that it would be useless to investigate Sujiatun at this point because it would be easy for the military to transfer several thousand people to some other camp in a single day. He also stated that most Falun Gong practitioners being used for organ pillaging were being detained in jails, labour camps and detention centres. The Jiutai district, Jilin Province, alone had detained more than 14,000 practitioners. The largest camp, 672-S, housed more than 120,000 prisoners, including large numbers of practitioners. The witness felt that the party-state saw adherents as "class enemies". The usual procedures and laws did not apply to them; they were treated as a commodity to fulfill economic development requirements, however ruthless it might be.[15]

**April 4:** The Coalition to Investigate the Persecution of Falun Gong in China (CIPFG) was formed as an investigation group to gather all possible leads in order to expose the inside stories of labour camps, prisons and hospitals that were colluding with one another in the persecution and illegal organ harvesting of practitioners.

Calls were made to several major hospitals and organ transplant centres in Hubei, Shanghai, Liaoning, Beijing, and Shaanxi to investigate. All had one similarity in their replies. There would be large amounts of donors before the end of April, and then the number of donors would be drastically reduced after that. Information surfaced that many hospitals and transplant centres were speeding their transplantation operations, suggesting that the Party was going all out to destroy all material evidence and witnesses.

**April 13:** Gao Zhisheng applied to join the CIPFG.

The party-state continued to deploy a force to suppress voices advocating dignity for all and the rule of law in China. One is Gao Zhisheng, a three time Nobel Peace Prize-nominated lawyer in the tradition of Nelson Mandela and Mahatma Gandhi. At one point, he was named one of China's top ten lawyers by the Ministry of Justice in Beijing. Party agents released its full wrath, however, when Gao, a Christian, decided to defend Falun Gong practitioners and document their persecution. Suppression began and he was convicted on a subversion charge.

*April 14*: Led by local officials, a U.S. delegation toured the facilities in Sujiatun and announced that nothing was found. This was entirely unsurprising, given that the tour took place more than six weeks after the initial allegation.

*April 16:* The World Organization to Investigate the Persecution of Falun Gong (WOIPFG) published its third report, revealing that military and quasi-military hospitals in several provinces were participating in the organ harvesting of practitioners.

*April 24:* Eighty-one members of the U.S. Congress cosigned a letter urging President Bush to initiate a full investigation into the organ harvesting charges and seek an explanation from Chinese leader Hu Jintao and an agreement to allow onsite third-party investigations.

*April 30:* The veteran military doctor living inside China sent out another letter, revealing the actual process of harvesting practitioners' organs. He said that the numbers of underground organ selling were many times greater than the numbers officially published by the CCP, and that attention of any investigation should be on military facilities.

*May 8:* Human rights lawyer, David Matas, and Canada's former Secretary of State (Asia Pacific), David Kilgour, announced that they would be carrying out an independent investigation into the allegations of organ harvesting of practitioners, a new crime against humanity and one completely contrary to the traditional values of the Chinese.

*May 21:* The Vice President of the EU, Edward McMillan-Scott, went to China to question two practitioners about the persecution of their movement. The facilitator was arrested and deported. Both practitioners were also arrested afterwards.

*July 6:* The Matas-Kilgour investigation report was published and became accessible in 18 languages at www.organharvestinvestigation.net. It affirmed large scale organ seizures from unwilling Falun Gong prisoners of conscience for profit. The authors said that from the official statistics published by the Chinese authorities, over 41,500 organ donations were unaccounted for and might have come from Falun Gong detainees. Such an atrocity was widely spread and was continuing.

In 2006, the Transplantation Society, based internationally in Montreal, opposed both the transplantation of organs from prisoners and the presentations of studies from China involving patient data or samples from recipients of organs or tissues from prisoners.

2007: *January:* The Matas-Kilgour report of 2006 July was updated.

In 2007, the World Medical Association (WMA) entered into an agreement with the Chinese Medical Association that organs of prisoners and other individuals in custody must not be used for transplantation except for members of their immediate family.

Dr. Francis L. Delmonico, director of medical affairs for The Transplantation Society (TTS) and an advisor to the World Health Organization (WHO), said to Chinese health officials: "It is vitally important that the Chinese have transparency of practice, including evidence that organs from prisoners were obtained with written, non-coercive permission, and continuing use of approved transplant centers and newly credentialed surgeons only. ..."[16]

In 2007/2008, the U.N. Rapporteur on Torture, Manfred Nowak, and the U.N. Rapporteur on Religious Intolerance asked the Government of China to explain the discrepancy between the number of Chinese transplants and the number of sources it was willing to acknowledge. It failed to respond substantively. The U.N. Committee Against Torture added its own consternation in its November 2008 report on China. Since then, there has been a much broader expression of concern to take every necessary step to avoid complicity in human rights violations during organ transplants in China.

Why did Beijing's party-state continue to refuse to disclose both death penalty and transplant statistics? One possible answer is that if these statistics were to become publicly accessible, the discrepancy between the number of transplants and the number of prisoners sentenced to death and executed would then become obvious. The party-state would be hard pressed not to account for the discrepancy once this information had been disclosed.

2009:  **July:** Independent researcher and author, Ethan Gutmann, calculated that 450,000 to 1 million practitioners were being held in labour camps, prison camps and other long-term detention facilities at any given time.[17]

**November:** A book titled *Bloody Harvest* by Matas and Kilgour was released. Their conclusions were formed from the cumulative effect of ultimately 52 different kinds of proof. "Each is verifiable in itself and most are incontestable. In combination, they constitute a clearly demonstrated pattern of systematic criminal wrongdoing in a country which lacks both the rule of law and independent judges".

2011:  An Amnesty International report stated: The authorities renewed the campaign to "transform" ... practitioners, which required prison and detention centres to force Falun Gong inmates to renounce their beliefs. Those considered "stubborn," that is, those who refuse to sign a statement to this effect, are typically tortured until they co-operate; many die in detention or shortly after release.


## A Better Way Forward

At a forum held at the margins of the annual assembly of the World Medical Association in Montevideo, Uruguay on October 13, 2011, David Kilgour stressed that the use of executed prisoners as a source of organs in China is an abhorrent practice because people are clearly being killed for the purpose of providing organs for others. Among many consequences, this violates elemental human dignity and delays the development of ethical strategies for recovering organs through informed and authentic consent across China.

Since transplant medicine is controlled by the Chinese government, it is responsible for these practices. Hence, the prevailing situation needs a determined and concerted response directed at the Chinese government for the good of the entire medical discipline worldwide.

David Kilgour called upon the international medical community to suspend the membership of the Chinese Medical Association in the WMA and to speak with one voice by calling for a boycott by medical journals of articles on transplantation from China, boycotting medical conferences held in China on transplantation, refusing to provide training in transplant medicine for doctors from China, suspending memberships of Chinese doctors in other biomedical bodies due to non-compliance with the organizations' ethical standards, and taking a position on pharmaceutical companies doing clinical trials in China relating to transplantation.

One of World Medicine's greatest achievements in the 20th century was its Code of Ethics. This code, the strongest foundation for patient-focused medicine in the 21st century, needs to be enforced in China. The best response from the medical community would be to speak up now.

All of us should be making concerted efforts to encourage our own national governments to develop a treaty that would ban profit from the products of human origin.

No action is too strong to discourage a barbaric practice which violates both the foundation of human dignity – respect for the human body – and the essence of ethical standards in medicine.

1   Accessed on 12-02-23 http://www.clearwisdom.net/html/cate-191/

2   "Brutal persecution suffered by women Falun Gong practitioners in China," Accessed on 12-02-16 www.clearwisdom.net/html/articles/2011/10/4/Zip.html#128512

3   McGregor, Richard. *The Party: the secret world of China's communist rulers* (New York: Harper Collins, 2010) page 167.

4   Matas, David and David Kilgour. *Bloody Harvest: The killing of Falun Gong for their organs* (Seraphim Editions, 2009) pages 42-43, and page 51.

5   Matas, David and David Kilgour. *Bloody Harvest: The killing of Falun Gong for their organs.* (Seraphim Editions, 2009)

6   Matas, David and David Kilgour. *Bloody Harvest: The killing of Falun Gong for their organs* (Seraphim Editions, 2009) page 56.

7   "The Bellagio Task Force Report on Transplantation, Bodily Integrity, and the International Traffic in Organs," Accessed on 12-02-16 www.icrc.org Transplant Proceedings (1997; 29: 2739-45).

8   Craig, Olga. Focus "The Butchers of Beijing," *Sunday Telegraph*, March 1, 1998.

9   Jefferies, David E. "Executions top 1,200 in one year," *South China Morning Post*, March 24, 2001. Accessed on 12-02-16 www.scmp.com.

10  Scheper-Huges, Nancy. "Postmodern cannibalism: black market trade of human organs," July 29, 2000.

11  Investigation Lead: People's Liberation Army General Logistics Department Responsible for Harvesting Organs from Living Falun Gong Practitioners [11/29/2009] Accessed on 12-02-15.

12  Ibid.

13  Coalition to Investigate the Persecution of Falun Gong in China. "Background" August, 2006. Accessed on 12-02-15.

14  Ibid.

15  Coalition to Investigate the Persecution of Falun Gong in China. "About Organ Harvesting," August, 2006. Accessed on 12-02-15.

16  Investigation Lead: People's Liberation Army General Logistics Department Responsible for Harvesting Organs from Living Falun Gong Practitioners [11/29/2009] Accessed on 12-02-15.

17  Coalition to Investigate the Persecution of Falun Gong in China. "Timeline of Important Events," August, 2006. Accessed on 12-02-15.

# The Impact of the Use of Organs from Executed Prisoners in China on the New Organ Transplantation Law in Israel

JACOB LAVEE, MD

In 2005, I was approached one day by a patient of mine with an unusual message. This patient had been continuously hospitalized in my department for more than one year with severe heart failure and had been a top priority candidate on the Israeli waiting list for heart transplantation. He reported to me he was fed up with the endless wait for a suitable heart donor and was told by his medical insurance company to go to China in two weeks' time as he was scheduled to undergo heart transplantation on a specific date. When asked how such an operation could be scheduled ahead of time, the patient responded he did not bother to inquire. The patient, indeed, went to China and underwent the operation on the exact date as promised ahead of time.

This was the first time I had been made aware of the possibility of undergoing heart transplantation in China as no Israeli patient had ever gone there for this operation before. For years, I have heard stories from my kidney transplant colleagues about Israeli patients going to China to get kidney transplants and, never bothering really to inquire, it was my assumption that the source of these kidneys was poor people selling one of their kidneys in order to improve their economic status. The fact that you can also get a heart transplant in China and, moreover, get it on a specific pre-scheduled date was a total surprise to me and got me researching.

It did not take me long to find out the gruesome details of the abhorrent Chinese practice used since the 1980s, whereby the source of most of the transplanted organs are prisoners sentenced to death or prisoners of conscience, whose consent is either non-existent or ethically invalid and whose demise might be timed for the convenience of the waiting recipient who could afford the cost of buying an organ. When I started my research in 2005, this practice was still officially denied by the Chinese authorities. Therefore the sources of information were mainly the testimony of Dr. Wang Guoqi, a former doctor in the Police Tianjin General Brigade Hospital, who fled to the U.S. and spoke in a hearing before the subcommittee on International Operations and Human Rights of the Committee on International Relations, House of Representatives, in June 2001.[1] As I was about to publish my research findings, Dr. Jiefu Huang, Vice Minister of Health of the People's Republic of China (PRC), publicly admitted for the first time in December 2005 that apart from a small portion of traffic victims, most of the cadaveric organs in China came from executed prisoners, albeit claiming that the only prisoners who were subject to capital punishment in the PRC are convicted criminals and that prisoners or their family provided informed consent for donation of organs after execution.

The results of my research were first published in October 2006 in the *Journal of the Israeli Medical Association*,[2] and I have added a call for the cessation of the Israeli participation in the process as I have found out that, of all transplant tourists gathering to China from all over the world to get organs, Israeli patients were probably the only ones fully reimbursed by their insurance companies. I have referred to this reimbursement as providing de facto recognition of the Chinese transplant activities as being legal and ethical and have called upon Israeli authorities to immediately ban it all together and denounce any Israeli participation in the atrocious process.

On July 2006, when my paper had already been sent for publication, Matas and Kilgour published their first version of the *Bloody Harvest* report, and I had therefore published an extended version of my original plea in another Israeli medical journal,[3] this time adding the chilling information regarding the use of executed Falun Gong practitioners as a major source of organs in China. Following the publication of these papers, the Israeli lay press picked up my call, and an extensive investigative story of the trade in executed prisoners' organs in China was published in Israel's most widespread newspaper.

An Op-ed on the same topic which I had published in the most popular local news portal *YNet* and a follow-up TV report all contributed to the public awareness of the issue.

Together with my friend and associate to the public campaign, the transplant surgeon Prof. Eytan Mor, we convened in June 2007 a special conference on ethical dilemmas in solving the organ shortage in Israel under the auspices of Israel's National Transplant Center and the Israel Society of Transplantation. Among the invited speakers were Prof. Francis Delmonico, then a special advisor on transplantation to the World Health Organization; Amnon Vidan, director of the Israeli branch of Amnesty International; Dr. Yoram Blashar, then chairman of Israel Medical Association; Prof. Gabriel Danovitch, renowned director of the kidney transplant program at UCLA Medical Center, and David Matas who gave the large audience a summary of the *Bloody Harvest* report. A day before the planned conference, we found ourselves in the midst of a diplomatic incident when we were asked by our Ministry of Health to consider cancelling Matas' presentation in response to a request forwarded by the Chinese embassy to our Ministry of Foreign Affairs. We rejected this request and were henceforth kindly asked to at least balance his presentation with a presentation by a representative of the Chinese embassy in Israel in order to avoid diplomatic discomfort. This presentation was indeed delivered in which the source of organs in China was not mentioned at all and the *Bloody Harvest* report was portrayed as just an attempt to slander China. The Chinese speaker was literally booed by the audience.

An interesting and unexpected public support to my call, at that time, came from one of the most respected rabbis in Israel, Rabbi Shalom Elyashiv, who has traditionally headed the minority of orthodox rabbis who ruled against accepting brain death as a legitimate form of death and hence, object to organ donation following brain death. While usually permissive of accepting organ donation from gentile donors who have been proclaimed brain dead, Rabbi Elyashiv surprised many when he openly declared that the use of organs from executed prisoners in China and the selling of those organs to anybody who could afford it was considered by Judaism as a form of God's desecration and should be avoided by all means, even if its avoidance would result in the death of the potential candidate for transplantation.

Following the intensive public discussion, a special meeting of the Health Committee of the Israeli Parliament convened to which representatives of all stakeholders were invited including candidates for organ transplantation, transplant physicians, directors of insurance companies and HMOs, Israeli Falun Gong practitioners and the Ministry of Health. After hearing all sides, the committee unanimously expressed its revulsion of the abhorrent practice in China and issued a call to stop sending Israeli patients for organ transplantation to China.

The committee went further, and together with the Ministry of Health, made sure that the new Organ Transplant Law, which was formulated during the same time, included a unique chapter[4] which bans any reimbursement of organ transplantation performed abroad if it involved illegal organ procurement or organ trade. The new law was passed into legislation by the Parliament in March 2008 and, shortly afterwards, rules were issued ordering all Israeli insurance companies to stop reimbursing any organ transplants performed in countries in which illegal organ procurement or organ trade are known to take place. These rules were immediately implemented by the insurance companies which brought transplant tourism from Israel to China to a complete and abrupt halt. These rules have also helped minimize the total number of transplant tourists from Israel to other venues in the world, cutting this number from 155 in 2006 to only 26 patients in 2011.

The Israeli Organ Transplant Law does not only close the gates for transplant tourism from Israel. In parallel, it includes several unique clauses which pave new ways to increase national organ donation, both from deceased and from living related donors, and thereby promotes national self-sufficiency in organ donation as highlighted by the Declaration of Istanbul.[5] Based on my recommendation to the steering committee of the Israeli National Transplant Center, the law has adopted a unique new policy granting priority in organ allocation to candidates who have been previously registered donors.[6] This unprecedented organ allocation policy was aimed towards abolishing the "free riders" phenomenon of candidates for organ transplantation who, for various reasons, object to organ donation and is based on the ethics principal of reciprocal altruism.

Other aspects of the law provide modest reimbursements for living donors which serve to remove disincentives to living donation.

These include the following non-fungible benefits reimbursements to any live donor who has been authorized by the Ethics Committee, all made by the government: earning loss reimbursement of 40 days, based on the donor's average income during the last 3 months prior to donation (an unemployed donor will be reimbursed according to the minimum salary in the market at the time of donation); a fixed sum transportation refund to cover all commuting to and from the hospital for the donor and his relatives for the entire hospitalization and follow-up period; a 7 day recovery reimbursement within 3 months after donation; five years reimbursement of medical, work capability loss and life insurance, all to be refunded upon submission of appropriate insurance policies and payment receipts, and reimbursement of five psychological consultations and treatments upon submission of appropriate receipts. All these measures have already borne fruits as organ donation, during 2011, has significantly increased by 68% compared to 2010.

Influencing any country to change its unethical and immoral conduct in organ retrieval and transplantation is a daunting task, especially in an enormous and secluded country like China. No single measure can be expected to make this shift and it is only through concerted variety of global efforts aimed at different levels of the atrocious chain which provides organs from executed prisoners and Falun Gong practitioners to wealthy candidates for organ transplantation from all over the world or even to local citizens, before this chain can hopefully be disassembled. The Israeli legal approach has successfully managed to disengage Israeli candidates for organ transplantation from getting their organs in China. If similar measures are enforced by other countries whose patients flock to China to receive their organs, there is a good chance that dwindling this major financial source will ultimately contribute to the dismantling of this widely condemned chain.

---

1 "Organs for Sale: China's growing trade and ultimate violation of prisoners' rights," Hearing before the subcommittee on International Operations and Human Rights of the Committee on International Relations, House of Representatives, June 27, 2001. Viewed at: http://commdocs.house.gov/committees/intlrel/hfa73452.000/hfa73452_0f.htm

2  Lavee J. "Organ transplantation using organs taken from executed prisoners in China – a call for the cessation of Israeli participation in the process," [Hebrew] Harefuah. 2006;145:749-52

3  Lavee J. "Shooting and cutting," [Hebrew]. *Medicine Cardiology.* 2:12-15, 2007. Viewed at: http://www.themedical.co.il/Upload/Magazines/Documents/23/medicine%20heart2.pdf

4  Israel Transplant Law - Organ Transplant Act, 2008. Viewed at: http://www.declarationofistanbul.org/index.php?option=com_content&view=article&id=267:israel-transplant-law-organ-transplant-act-2008&catid=83:legislation&Itemid=130

5  The Declaration of Istanbul. Viewed at: http://www.declarationofistanbul.org/

6  Lavee J, Ashkenazi T, Gurman G, Steinberg D. "A new law for allocation of donor organs in Israel," *Lancet* (2010): 375(9720):1131-3

# How Should the Academic Community Respond to the Continued Use of Executed Prisoners as a Source of Organs for Transplantation in China?

GABRIEL DANOVITCH, MD

The concept, now taken for granted, that biomedical research must comply with accepted ethical standards has become normative in the decades since the promulgation of the Declaration of Helsinki. The Declaration itself was a response to the gross abrogation of basic human rights that occurred in the process of medical experimentation in Nazi Germany and later in the clinical trials in Tuskegee and elsewhere. The Declaration of Helsinki has thus become part of the "bone-marrow" of clinical researchers just as the Hippocratic Oath is, or should be, part of the bone-marrow of all engaged in clinical practice. All clinical research has to comply with the Declaration of Helsinki before it can be considered for publication in medical journals or presented at medical meetings. Manuscripts and abstracts are routinely submitted to an "ethics filter".

The practice of obtaining organs for transplantation from executed prisoners has been widely regarded as an unacceptable abrogation of human rights for decades. It was not until 2007 that expression of abhorrence of the practice and a series of practical steps to respond were published in a respected academic journal on behalf of professional transplant society – The Transplantation Society (TTS). Yet, despite international condemnation, including recognition by highly placed government officials of the People's Republic of China, that the practice is unacceptable and does not conform to international standards, it continues unabated.

The last decade has seen a welcomed sea-change in the nature of interaction between China and the rest of the world on many levels, such that it is hard to recall the near isolation of that great country a mere generation ago. Medical research from China commonly reaches the English-speaking world, medical exchange and training is common, and pharmaceutical companies do business on a massive level and conduct drug-development and clinical research. These normative and welcome interactions are now accompanied for the first time by submission of reports of organ transplant-related clinical experience and clinical research where the "donor" source has been executed prisoners. How should the academic transplant community respond to such submissions?

At the July 2010 biennial World Transplant Congress meeting of TTS in Vancouver over 30 abstracts were submitted from China and considered for acceptance, with data from several hundreds of transplants, where the donor source was deemed likely to be executed prisoners. This occurred despite the fact that a standard ethics filter mechanism was in place, and the TTS ethics policy regarding organs from executed prisoners had been published and was well-known. Fortunately the failure of the ethics filter to prevent acceptance of these abstracts was recognized, and authors were specifically required to state, in the text of their abstracts, as a condition of acceptance, that no data from studies using executed donor organs were included. As a result, most abstracts were withdrawn.

In the August 2010 issue of the *American Journal of Transplantation,* Allam et al[1] reported on the complications suffered by patients returning to Saudi Arabia and Egypt after liver transplantation in China. The authors commented that "the main growing concern with this choice (i.e. travel to China for liver transplantation) was the uncertainty regarding the outcome". In an accompanying editorial, also concerned mainly with recipient complications, only passing reference was made to the actual source of the organs – executed prisoners who had suffered "severe brain injury in all cases" followed by "donation after cardiac death (DCD)".[2]

In the October 2010 issue of *Liver Transplantation,* the official journal of the American Society for the Study of Liver Diseases (AASLD) and the International Liver Transplantation Society (ILTS), lead author Zhi-Jun Zhu et al from Tianjin First Central Hospital reported on the feasibility of using a liver infected with the fluke Clonorchis sinensis for liver transplantation in fourteen cases.[3] In the methods section of the article the authors reported that the livers were harvested *"using the standard DCD (Donation after Cardiac Death) donor organ procurement technique"*. An accompanying editorial commented only on the technical aspects of the report and ignored the donor source.[4]

These overtly benign statements of the source of transplanted organs obscure the fact that deceased donor organ recovery in China involves death by execution and that those euphemistically described as "donating" their organs were prisoners, whose "severe brain injury" was most likely a result of execution by a gun-shot to the head. It is difficult to know for sure how many such "donation by execution" take place in China but it is safe to say that the numbers provided by the official China Liver Transplant Registry (www.cltr.org.en), which reported close to 19,000 cases in the period between January 1993 and July 2010, are likely to represent a low estimate. There may be many more.

In an editorial commentary[5] on the publication of data obtained from transplants where executed prisoners were the donor source, a series of options for action by the professional transplant community was proposed. These included:

▸ International and national professional medical societies and journals should not accept abstracts, publications or presentations from Chinese transplant centers unless the authors clearly indicate that the data presented is in concordance with the most recent Chinese government regulations regarding transplant tourism and that executed prisoners were not the source of organs.

▸ Membership of international professional societies by Chinese transplant professionals must be conditioned by acceptance of ethics policies that specifically express the unacceptability of executed prisoners as a source of organs.

▸ Pharmaceutical companies must ensure that no executed prisoners are the source of organs used in their studies and that Chinese government regulations regarding transplant tourism are adhered to rigorously.

▸ Training of Chinese transplant professionals by the international community must be conditioned on commitments that trainees will not engage, directly or indirectly, in the use of organs from executed prisoners.

The response by the editorial board of the *American Journal of Transplantation* was most gratifying. Routinely included, since May 2011, in the instructions to authors submitting manuscripts to these journals is the following statement:

> The *American Journal of Transplantation* (AJT) will not accept manuscripts whose data derives from transplants involving organs obtained from executed prisoners. Manuscripts writing about this practice (e.g. an editorial or a report recounting the secondary consequences of this practice) may be considered at the discretion of the Editorial Board, but require a written appeal to the Board prior to submission of the manuscript.

In October 2011, the *Lancet* published an editorial letter entitled "Time for a boycott of Chinese science and medicine pertaining to organ transplantation".[6] The prestigious *Journal of Clinical Investigation* published a specific editorial position statement regarding publication of articles on human organ transplantation opening with the following statement[7]:

> The practice of transplanting organs from executed prisoners in China appears to be widespread. We vigorously condemn this practice and, effective immediately, will not consider manuscripts on human organ transplantation for publication unless appropriate non-coerced consent of the donor is provided and substantiated.

Other steps have been taken. The website of the Declaration of Istanbul on organ Trafficking and Transplant Tourism (www.declarationofistanbul.org) includes a document on Policy for Meeting Content which includes the following statement:

> All abstract submission forms should include a statement to the effect that 'The authors attest that (a) all data (clinical finding, description of clinical material, etc.) were derived from research and clinical activities carried out in accordance with the Principles of the Declaration of Istanbul and (b) executed prisoners were not the source of organs and tissues in any of the activities reported.'

This policy was included in the instructions for abstract submission at the International Society for Organ Donation and Procurement (ISODP) meeting in Buenos Aires in November 2011 and at the World Transplant Congress in Berlin in July 2012.

It should be emphasized that it is not the intent of these policies to prevent academic discussion of controversial issues in organ transplantation in China or elsewhere. Rather the intent is to provide succor to those in China who wish to see positive change. In this respect, to their credit, some Chinese Ministry of Health officials have indicated their intention to end the practice and pilot projects with the use of brain dead donors and conventional DCD donors are underway.[8] Yet the use of executed prisoner organs continues, with no clear evidence of abatement. But expressions of good intentions are not enough. In the professional transplant community, it is not adequate to merely give lip service to our repugnance. We cannot control events in China, but, at the very least, we can control the content of our meetings and journals and work towards the day when Chinese organ transplantation will take its place as an honored and respected member of the international organ transplant community.

1 Allam, N., M. Al Saghier, Y. el Sheikh, et al. "Clinical outcomes for Saudi and Egyptian patients receiving deceased donor liver transplantation China," Am J Transplant 10 (2010): 1834-1841.

2 Fung, J. "The sleeping giant awakens—liver transplantation in China," Am J Transplant 10 (2010): 1723-1724.

3 Zhi-Jun Zhu, Zhong-Yang Shen, Wei Gao, et al. "Feasibility of Using a Liver Infected with Clonorchis sinensis for Liver Transplantation:Fourteen Cases," Liver Transplant 16 (2010): 1440-1444

4 Kotton, C., R.Hurtado. "Not Just a Fluke: Expanding the Organ Supply," Liver Transplant 16 (2010): 1343

5 Danovitch, G., M. Shapiro, J. Lavee. "The Use of Executed Prisoners as a Source of Organs Transplants in China Must Stop," Am J Transplant 11 (2011):426-428.

6 Caplan, A., G.M. Danovitch, M. Epstein, J. Lavee, M. Shapiro. "Time for a boycott of Chinese science and medicine pertaining to organ transplantation," Lancet (2011) 378;1218

7 Caplan, A., H. Rockman, L. Turka, "Editorial position on publishing articles on human organ transplantation," J Clin Invest. 122, 1 (2012):2.

8 Huang, J., J. Millis, M. Miliis, et al. "A pilot programme of organ donation after cardiac death in China," Lancet 379 (2012):862-865.

# Responsibilities of International Pharmaceutical Companies in the Abusive Chinese Organ Transplant System

ARNE SCHWARZ

*The abuse in China has to be of concern to the global community because it is a grave human rights violation and because the developed world has been complicit in the abuse.*

— David Matas[1]

After the United States, China is the country with the most organ transplantations worldwide.

The Chinese organ transplant system, however, does not fully comply with the ethical standards for organ transplants agreed on by the global medical community. The World Health Organization, the World Medical Association, The Transplantation Society and even the Chinese Medical Association have agreed in many official statements on ethical standards for organ transplantations, yet these standards have not completely been implemented in the Chinese organ transplant system. Thus this system has been and still continues to be abusive.

From the first organ transplants in the early 1970s right up to 2005, the Chinese government has tried to hide the fact that nearly all organs for transplantations have been procured from prisoners.[2] Voluntary organ donations by free citizens have always been extremely rare in China for cultural reasons, but a lack of transparency and a lack of trust in the abusive and commercialized transplant system have also been contributing factors.[3]

In 2008, the Chinese Vice Minister of Health admitted in the medical journal *The Lancet*:

> In China, more than 90% of transplanted organs are obtained from executed prisoners.[4]

According to statistics by the Chinese Ministry of Health presented in 2010 at a transplant conference in Madrid, more than 100,000 kidneys, livers, hearts, lungs and pancreases had been transplanted in China from 1997-2008. The Chinese Vice Minister of Health confirmed at this conference that still

> ... over 90% of grafts from deceased donors are from executed prisoners. ... a source that does not comply with international ethical and standard of practice.[5]

This means that by now more than 100,000 prisoners' organs have been used for transplantations in China – a figure made possible only because China executes each year more prisoners than all other countries combined worldwide. Prisoners are condemned to death for even minor offenses, and the Chinese legal system is far from complying with international standards for fair trials. The actual number of prisoners executed each year is a state secret in China.

But the global medical community strictly opposed the use of prisoners' organs for transplants. The World Medical Association (WMA) says in its "Statement on Human Organ Donation and Transplantation":

> Free and informed decision making is a process requiring the exchange and understanding of information and the absence of coercion. Because prisoners and other individuals in custody are not in a position to give consent freely and can be subject to coercion, their organs must not be used for transplantation except for members of their immediate family.[6]

The Chinese Medical Association (CMA) also agreed with this WMA statement in 2007.[7]

The use of prisoner organs for transplantation was condemned by the WMA as early as 1985[8] and has continued to be reported in detail by western NGOs[9] and newspapers for over twenty years, raising increased international concern.[10] This concern became even more urgent in 2006 when a report by independent Canadian investigators David Kilgour and David Matas presented compelling evidence that organs from prisoners of conscience were used for transplantations in China as well.[11]

Outsiders perceive the abusive organ transplantations in China usually as rogue Chinese practices. However, it has been ignored how deeply transplant surgeons and transplant units of other countries, as well as some international pharmaceutical companies, have been involved in the abusive Chinese transplant system.

Many leading Chinese surgeons have received their transplantology training in transplant units of western countries including the UK, the U.S., Australia, Canada and Germany.[12] And western transplant surgeons serve as advisors for the Chinese transplant system or cooperate with it.[13]

The involvement of international pharmaceutical companies in the Chinese transplant system is also significant. Some of these pharmaceutical companies test, promote and sell their immunosuppressive drugs in China very actively despite knowing that the Chinese transplant system does not fully comply with international ethical standards.

Immunosuppressive drugs are needed to prevent the rejection of transplanted organs. These anti-rejection drugs are essential for the success of transplantations in many countries. The market for these drugs is very profitable since the drugs are expensive and needed for the rest of a patient's life. The Chinese market for immunosuppressive drugs is already huge but still has a much greater potential. While other markets for anti-rejection drugs are shrinking after patents expire, the Chinese market is still expanding.[14]

The first hint of the involvement of a pharmaceutical company in the abusive Chinese transplant system was given in the comprehensive report *Organ Procurement and Judicial Execution in China* published in 1994 by the NGO Human Rights Watch. It emphasized the importance of immunosuppressive drugs for the "boost of the Chinese transplant program":

> From 1983 onwards, two unrelated factors combined to give a major boost to the (organ transplant) program: first, the commencement of

a series of "crackdown on crime" (yan-da) campaigns, held every year since 1983, which greatly increased the number of criminals sentenced to death and hence the potential supply of transplantable organs; and second, the introduction to China of Cyclosporine A, an acknowledged "wonder drug" which greatly raised the success rate in transplant operations. ... Cyclosporine A (CsA), an immunosuppressive agent which inhibits the body's natural tendency to reject foreign body tissue, was introduced into China in the mid-1980s, apparently by the Swiss company Sandoz. ... The vast majority of kidney transplant patients in China now receive expensive follow-up treatment involving CsA therapy.[15]

Later on, other international pharmaceutical companies such as Novartis, Roche, Astellas, Wyeth, Pfizer and most recently, the Canadian company Isotechnika,[16] have started to use the Chinese market opportunities for immunosuppressive drugs with their own anti-rejection drugs.

One may wonder whether some of the pharmaceutical companies have taken advantage of the under-regulated Chinese transplant market or even "boosted" the prisoner-based organ transplant system through their business.

Some of these pharmaceutical companies do not only promote and sell their immunosuppressive drugs in China but also hold clinical trials in Chinese hospitals for studying the effects of their anti-rejection drugs with patients who received transplanted organs.

Several pharmaceutical companies have recently begun clinical trials involving hundreds of transplant patients:

- June 2004: Wyeth (now Pfizer) began a trial involving 122 transplanted kidneys.

- January 2005: Novartis began a trial involving approximately 300 transplanted kidneys.

- 2006: Roche began a trial involving 36 transplanted hearts.

- March 2007: Astellas began a trial involving 42 transplanted livers.

- July 2007: Astellas began a trial involving 240 transplanted kidneys.

- January 2008: Astellas began a trial involving 172 transplanted livers.

- April 2008: Roche began a trial involving about 90 transplanted livers.

- September 2008: Roche began a trial involving approximately 210 transplanted kidneys.

- December 2010: Pfizer began a trial involving 24 transplanted kidneys.[17]

These 9 registered clinical trials totalling approximately 1,200 transplanted organs were conducted in more than 20 civil and military Chinese hospitals. There is compelling circumstantial evidence that at least in two of these hospitals, organs belonging to prisoners of conscience from the banned Falun Gong spiritual movement were used for transplantation.[18]

There are approximately 40 more registered clinical transplant trials with more than 2,000 transplanted organs in a multitude of Chinese hospitals using anti-rejection drugs of some of these companies, though the "responsible party" for these trials are Chinese university or military hospitals.[19]

The critical question in this context is: While more than 90% of all transplanted organs in China came from prisoners, where did the approximately 1,200 transplanted organs used in these clinical trials come from?

Aside from selling and testing anti-rejection drugs in China, Roche has also been producing its immunosuppressive drug CellCept in China since 2006 in a new 15 million Euro factory built in Shanghai. Asked by a newspaper why Roche produces this drug specifically in China, Roche CEO and later Chairman of the Board of Directors Franz Humer reasoned:

> ... contrary to Japan, in China there were no ethical or cultural stoppages for transplant medicine.[20]

Indeed, the abusive Chinese transplant system is not stopped by ethical or cultural considerations and uses prisoner organs because Chinese citizens are not willing to donate organs voluntarily. The popular Chinese newspaper *Global Times* writes:

> Chinese tradition does not allow for bodies to be damaged in any way after death. It is emotionally unacceptable for donors' relatives to see part of the donor's body being cut out or taken away by strangers. ...[21]

And in 2009 the Chinese magazine *Caijing* wrote:

> Fewer than 30 of the approximately 20,000 human organ transplants in China over the past two years were donated by citizen-patients. The vast majority were harvested from the bodies of executed criminals, according to Chen Zhonghua, deputy director of the Organ Transplant Society of the China Medical Association.[22]

The involvement of Roche and Astellas in the Chinese transplant system goes further. They cooperate with China to set up medical databases to improve the logistics of liver and kidney transplantations. They have been investing into the sponsorship of transplant activities in China.[23]

All these facts suggest that some of the pharmaceutical companies do business in China as they do elsewhere in the world despite the fact that most transplant organs in China are unethically procured from executed prisoners. Thus, one may wonder whether some of these pharmaceutical companies turn a blind eye on the abusive character of the Chinese transplant system for the sake of business opportunities and take the risk to undermine thereby global ethical standards.

In Switzerland, where the headquarters of Roche and Novartis are located, some politicians noticed this problem. Starting in 1998, and later in 2006 and 2008, members of the Swiss parliament asked the Swiss government critical questions about its attitude toward the rogue Chinese transplant system and the involvement of Swiss pharmaceutical companies Roche and Novartis.[24]

In September 2009, the author of this essay decided to do a case study about the transplant business of Swiss company Hoffmann-La Roche in China. He wrote a letter to the Roche Group Compliance Officer outlining the abusive character of the Chinese transplant system and asked how Roche had ensured that the approximately 300 transplanted organs in their three transplant trials in China didn't come from executed prisoners while statistically more than 90% of all transplanted organs in China came from prisoners.

Here is the essential part of Roche's lengthy reply letter:

> ... Roche is in no way in charge of the supply of organs. ... Roche is, as mentioned above, neither in China nor in any other country

of the world in charge of the supply of organs. Anonymity and privacy of the very personal donor data are protected by law. Roche is not entitled to know from where or from which donors the transplanted organs come. ...[25]

This reply is insufficient because it does not address that, contrary to all other countries of the world, the vast majority of all transplanted organs in China have been procured from executed prisoners. Therefore, due diligence and special safeguards are needed to ensure that transplanted organs in anti-rejection trials in China don't come from executed prisoners either. Pharmaceutical companies that perform clinical trials in China should ensure that transplants used in such trials are not sourced from executed prisoners, while at the same time the companies must also ensure that "personal anonymity and privacy" of donors and recipients are still protected. If the companies cannot meet these criteria, they should refrain from these market opportunities. Thus, living up to their corporate responsibilities, pharmaceutical companies could considerably strengthen their ethical credibility worldwide.

The *Guiding Principles on Human Cell, Tissue and Organ Transplantation* published by the World Health Organization, demand in Principle 10 the traceability of transplanted organs back to the donor and Principle 11 says:

> The organization and execution of donation and transplantation activities, as well as their clinical results, must be transparent and open to scrutiny, while ensuring that the personal anonymity and privacy of donors and recipients are always protected.[26]

The Transplantation Society, the leading international society of transplantologists, sponsored by Roche and other international pharmaceutical companies as Novartis and Astellas, recommends as ethical guideline for the interaction with transplant programs in China:

> Collaboration within clinical studies should only be considered if the study does not violate the Helsinki Declaration of the World Medical Association: Ethical Principles For Medical Research Involving Human Subjects, and does not violate the Policy and Ethics Statement of the Transplantation Society, for example through the involvement of recipients of organs or tissues from executed prisoners.[27]

And the United Nations Human Rights Council endorsed the *Guiding Principles on Business and Human Rights* emphasizing the

> ... corporate responsibility to respect human rights, which means that business enterprises should act with due diligence to avoid infringing on the rights of others and to address adverse impacts with which they are involved.[28]

In light of the stark contradictions between all these principles and Roche's answer, the author of this essay discussed the situation with some NGOs and shared with them the results of his research on clinical trials of international pharmaceutical companies. The responsibility of pharmaceutical companies for their transplant activities in China has now been addressed even further:

- In January 2010 the Swiss NGOs "Declaration of Berne" and Greenpeace Switzerland awarded to Roche the shame prize "Public Eye Swiss Award 2010" for irresponsible company practices because Roche

> ... conducts clinical studies in China of its immunosuppressive drug CellCept without being able to state the origin of donated organs ...

- Roche also received the negative prize "Public Eye People's Award" by the internet vote of 5,723 people worldwide. Both Awards got national and international media attention.[29]

- At the March 2010 annual shareholder meeting, Roche was heavily criticized for its transplant trials in China (Roche and Novartis had already been challenged in 2008 about their questionable sales of immunosuppressive drugs in China).[30]

- In August 2010, Amnesty International published a statement against the use of prisoner organs and appealed explicitly to pharmaceutical companies to respect human rights.[31]

- In August 2010, the NGO "Doctors Against Forced Organ Harvesting" appealed to pharmaceutical companies

> ... to set high standards in corporate responsibility ... refraining from using transplants that might be legally, but not ethically acceptable.[32]

- In August 2010, the Swiss newspaper *Le Temps* reported:

Novartis observes a moratorium for its clinical immunosuppressive drug trials in China. Its spokesman, Satoshi Sugimoto, declares that Novartis 'supports the public statement of Amnesty' and will work on bringing together the stakeholders for 'the next steps'.[33]

▸ At the August 2010 Congress of the Transplantation Society in Vancouver, David Matas addressed the responsibility of pharmaceutical companies.[34]

▸ In September 2010, the Triodos Bank, one of the world's leading sustainable banks, removed Roche from all its investments because Roche no longer met the bank's minimum standard for human rights:

Roche does not take full responsibility for its clinical trials in China. In our final assessment we balanced the gathered information and concluded that Roche's approach to clinical trials in China is not acceptable. The company's size and influence warrant a much clearer position on the origin of transplanted organs. Since the company no longer meets our human rights minimum standard, it has been excluded from the Triodos sustainable investment universe and will be removed from all Triodos investments within the short term.[35]

▸ The Dutch ASN bank also removed Roche immediately from its universe because

Roche cannot guarantee that the testing of drugs doesn't make use of organs from executed Chinese prisoners.[36]

▸ At the March 2011 shareholder meeting, Roche was again criticized for its transplant trials in China.[37]

▸ At a meeting during the American Transplant Congress in May 2011, David Matas presented an abundance of facts on "Anti-rejection Drug Trials and Sales in China." His data even suggested that Roche and Astellas conducted transplant trials at two Chinese hospitals where there is compelling evidence that organs of Falun Gong prisoners of conscience are used for transplantations.[38]

▸ At the same meeting, the senior medical director of a global clinical research organization took a stand against transplant trials in China.[39]

▸ Finally, in December 2011, U.S. Congressman Joe Pitts said in a floor speech:

... foreign companies are already making investments to benefit off of the thriving organ transplant market. Pharmaceutical companies like Roche and Isotechnika Pharma have been involved in clinical drug testing of transplant patients. A British firm, TFP Ryder Healthcare, is proposing a medical facility that would include an organ transplant center. Before they follow suit, U.S. companies must understand the unethical climate that exists in China. And our State Department and the U.N. must treat these actions as an abuse of China's international agreements and human rights of their own people.[40]

This broad opposition against unethical transplant trials in China shows an urgent need for a discussion of the responsibilities of pharmaceutical companies in a poorly regulated rogue business environment like the Chinese transplant system.

To **not do harm** is a fundamental principle of medical ethics based on the Hippocratic Oath.

With common therapies, this means not to do harm to the **treated patient.** For organ transplantations this should also mean not to do harm to the **person whose organ is used for transplantation.**

Another basic principle in medical ethics is to get informed and freely-given consent for the treatment. With common therapies this means informed **consent of the patient for his treatment.** For organ transplantations this also means the **freely given informed consent of the person whose organ is used for transplantation.**

Organ transplantation is a medical treatment, so the people in charge of this treatment like doctors, medical staff or the "responsible party" of clinical trials have the responsibility to not do harm to their patient but also to not do harm to the person from which the new organ for their patient is provided and to ensure that there is a freely-given informed consent for organ donation.

Of course, in such a complex medical treatment like organ transplantation, some duties and responsibilities have to be delegated. So in daily practice, the medical team that treats the patient and will transplant the organ is different from the team that retrieves the organ from the donor. The transplantation team delegates providing the organ to another team closer to the donor and hopefully less biased toward the donor's concerns. The ethical responsibility for providing the organ is delegated to this team.

This makes sense **as long as** the team treating the patient who needs an organ can be sure that the transplanted organ is provided according to international medical ethic standards. In many countries, transplanted organs are provided beyond reasonable doubt according to medical ethics. In these countries, the WHO Guiding Principles for Organ Transplantation are fully implemented. Transplanted organs can be traced back to their origin; the process of organ donation is transparent and open to scrutiny. There are strict laws on organ donation according to medical ethics. There are authorities to make sure the laws are observed. There are trustworthy institutions to organize organ donation according to laws and medical ethics. For example, the Swiss transplantation law gives access to medical records even to foreign authorities and international organizations; thus, it is possible to detect illegal organ trafficking or other infringements against this law.[41]

Not all of these conditions for a responsible delegation of organ procurement are met in China. *Thus, under these circumstances, delegating organ procurement to an abusive transplant system is irresponsible.*

According to the Chinese Ministry of Health, the majority of organs transplanted in China come from prisoners. All details about death penalty and executions are a state secret. Prisoners are executed more and more in the secrecy of so-called mobile "execution vans" with medical equipment.[42] International demands to investigate the allegations that organs are also procured from prisoners of conscience are declined. A considerable share of all transplantations is conducted under the special conditions of military hospitals.

**How is it possible that not only Chinese but also respected western transplant surgeons and pharmaceutical companies ignore all these facts and do business as usual?**

History, especially German history, shows that even respected institutions and personalities can be blindfolded on the problem of a rogue context for their activities. Bioscientists of the famous German scientific "Kaiser Wilhelm Gesellschaft" cooperated with and trusted in a rogue system as if it were a trustworthy one.

A research report of the worldwide respected German scientific "Max Planck Society," the successor of the Kaiser Wilhelm Gesellschaft, says about biosciences and Nazi crimes:

> In case of the biosciences culpable behavior could ... also develop because scientists claimed for themselves distance to

politics despite the rogue context surrounding them. Either, they neglected to inform themselves on the origin of their human cadaveric specimen and to pursue hints to the linkage with murderous Nazi politics. Or, they ignored their knowledge about the persecution and assassination of humans whose body parts they used for their experiments and felt entitled to pursue their research interests "on duty for scientific progress" irrespective of all moral limits.[43]

The Chinese transplant system poses a "rogue context" for transplant activities. Thus doctors, medical staff, *and* pharmaceutical companies have a special responsibility not to exploit such a "rogue context" for their activities and to protect vulnerable populations like prisoners. They have to ensure with due diligence that international ethical standards on organ donation are met in all their transplant activities as long as China's transplant system does not fully abide by the WHO Guiding Principles on Organ Transplantation.[43]

Of course, pharmaceutical companies cannot and should not stop delivering their life-saving immunosuppressive drugs to people who need them after having received a transplant organ.

But as long as: (a) organs still come from prisoners, (b) organs can not be traced back to their origin, (c) the process of organ procurement is not transparent and (d) the transplant system is not open to scrutiny, **international pharmaceutical companies should immediately stop clinical transplant trials in China, should not promote their transplant drugs for future transplantations in China and should insist on the full implementation of the WHO Guiding Principles on Organ Transplantation in China as condition for transplant cooperation with China.**

This essay is based on remarks by Arne Schwarz prepared for the "Human Rights and International Organ Transplantation Abuse" Conference of the International Society for Human Rights on September 30, 2010 in Geneva.

1 Kate Dennehy, "Unauthorised organ trade an ongoing evil,"
  *Brisbane Times*, 30 Oct 2010.
  http://www.brisbanetimes.com.au/queensland/unauthorised-organ-
  trade-an-ongoing-evil-20101030-177y7.html#ixzz1ompIKEAS

2 Zhonghua Klaus Chen, "A public seminar on: Current Situation of
  Organ Donation and Transplantation in China – from Stigma to
  Stigmata," City University of Hong Kong, 6 Dec 2007.
  http://www.cityu.edu.hk/garc/ARC/ARCfile/SSS/SSS06122007.htm
  Wang Ye "Prisoners' organs not harvested without consent,"
  *China Daily*, 11 Apr 2006. http://www.chinadaily.com.cn/
  china/2006-04/11/content_564719.htm

3 Laurie Burkit, "China to Stop Harvesting Inmate Organs,"
  *Wall Street Journal*, 23 Mar 2012.
  http://online.wsj.com/article/SB10001424052702304724404577729
  8661625345898.html

4 Jiefu Huang, et al. "Government policy and organ transplantation in
  China," *The Lancet*, 6 Dec 2008.
  http://www.thelancet.com/journals/lancet/article/PIIS0140-
  6736(08)61359-8/fulltext

5 Jiefu Huang, "Tomorrow's Organ Transplantation Program in China,"
  Presentation at the Madrid Conference on Organ Donation and
  Transplantation, 23-25 Mar 2010.

6 "WMA Statement on Human Organ Donation and Transplantation,"
  Oct 2006
  http://www.wma.net/en/30publications/10policies/t7/index.html

7 "Chinese Medical Association Reaches Agreement With World
  Medical Association Against Transplantation Of Prisoners's Organs,"
  *Medical News Today*, 7 Oct 2007.
  http://www.medicalnewstoday.com/releases/84754.php

8 Harold Hillman, "Harvesting organs from recently executed prisoners.
  Practice must be stopped," *British Medical Journal*, 24 Nov 2001.
  http://www.ncbi.nlm.nih.gov/pmc/articles/
  PMC1121712/?tool=pmcentrez

9 Amnesty International: "China: Death Penalty Action: Victims in
  their thousands: the Death penalty in 1992," 30 Jun 1993.
  http://www.amnesty.org/en/library/info/ASA17/009/1993/en
  An unusually comprehensive report with an abundance of facts and
  sources was presented by Human Rights Watch: "Organ Procurement
  and Judicial Execution in China," Aug 1994.

http://www.hrw.org/legacy/reports/1994/china1/china_948.htm
Laogai Research Foundation: "Harry Wu Leads Distinguished Panel
Before Congressional Committee," Sep 1996.
http://www.christusrex.org/www1/sdc/Sep96a.htm

10 Barbara Basler, "Kidney Transplants in China Raise Concern About
Source," *The New York Times*, 3 Jun 1991.
http://www.nytimes.com/1991/06/03/world/kidney-transplants-in-
china-raise-concern-about-source.html

Theresa Poole, "China's executioners work overtime: International
outcry over organ transplant grows as car thieves join rising toll of
those shot after summary trials," *The Independent*, 30 Oct 1994.
http://www.independent.co.uk/news/world/chinas-executioners-
work-overtime-international-outcry-over-organ-transplant-grows-as-car-
thieves-join-rising-toll-of-those-shot-after-summary-trials-1445746.html

11 David Matas and David Kilgour, *Bloody Harvest: The killing of Falun
Gong for their organs* (Seraphim Editions, 2009).
http://organharvestinvestigation.net/

12 Examples for prominent Chinese surgeons who got their transplant
training in Australia or the UK are Huang Jiefu, Shi Bingyi and
Chen Zhonghua.
http://chinavitae.com/biography/Huang_Jiefu/career
http://www.cuan.cn/engpro/WebExpertDetail.aspx?ID=703
http://www.cityu.edu.hk/garc/ARC/ARCfile/SSS/SSS06122007.htm

Also in Canada fellowship trainings for Chinese transplant surgeons
are offered.
http://www.lhsc.on.ca/Research_Training/MOTP/Fellowship_
Training/index.htm

13 Examples of western transplant centers with close connections to China
are the transplant section at the University of Chicago Medical Center
or the German Heart Institute Berlin.
http://supportucmc.uchicago.edu/site/c.phLWJ6PFKmG/
b.6444925/k.E6FC/UC_Surgeon_Helping_China_Modernize_its_
Organ_Procurement_System.htm
http://german.cri.cn/21/2005/11/04/1@39490.htm

14 http://www.drugs.com/news/double-digit-increase-sales-operating-
profit1-core-eps-18984.html

15 http://www.hrw.org/legacy/reports/1994/china1/china_948.htm

16 http://www.prnewswire.com/news-releases/3sbio-and-isotechnika-
pharma-announce-strategic-partnership-to-develop-and-commercialize-
voclosporin-in-china-101366344.html

17 http://clinicaltrials.gov/ for all trials but Roche 2006 heart trial found at http://www.roche-trials.com

18 David Matas, "Antirejection Drug Trials and Sales in China," American Transplant Congress Philadelphia, 30 Apr 2011. https://dafoh.org/Matas_speech.php

19 http://chictr.clinicaltrialecrf.org/en/

20 Oliver Stock, "Transplantationsbank China," *Handelsblatt*, 7 Nov 2005.
"...Warum er ausgerechnet dieses Medikament in Shanghai produzieren lasse, begründet Humer so: Im Gegensatz zu Japan gebe es in China keine ethischen oder kulturellen Hemmungen gegenüber der Transplantationsmedizin. ..."
http://www.handelsblatt.com/unternehmen/industrie/transplantationsbank-china%3B985748

21 Fu Wen, "Life after Death," *Global Times*, 31 Aug 2010.
http://www.globaltimes.cn/china/society/2010-08/568586.html

22 Jingjing Liu, et al. "Executed criminals supply most of the transplanted organs in China, fueling ethics debates and demand for live-donor surgery," *Caijing Magazine*, Sep 2009.
http://english.caijing.com.cn/2009-09-09/110243848.html

23 "China to set up databank for kidney patients in need of transplant," *People's Daily Online*, 13 Dec 2009.
http://english.peopledaily.com.cn/90001/90782/90880/6840394.html
Astellas China News, 14 Jun 2008.
http://www.astellas.com.cn/html/en/show.asp?ClassID=11&ContentID=54&LvID=4

24 http://www.parlament.ch/ab/frameset/d/n/4515/179578/d_n_4515_179578_179987.htm
http://www.parlament.ch/D/Suche/Seiten/geschaefte.aspx?gesch_id=20063349
http://www.parlament.ch/d/suche/seiten/geschaefte.aspx?gesch_id=20083197

25 Roche reply letter to the author of this essay, dated November 4, 2009:
"... Roche ist in keiner Art und Weise für die Beschaffung von Organen zuständig. ... Roche ist, wie oben erwähnt, weder in China noch in einem anderen Land der Welt für die Beschaffung von Organen zuständig. Anonymität und Vertraulichkeit der höchstpersönlichen Spenderdaten sind rechtlich geschützt; Roche hat keinen Anspruch,

zu erfahren, woher oder von welchen Spendern die transplantierten Organe stammen..."

26 http://apps.who.int/gb/ebwha/pdf_files/WHA63/A63_24-en.pdf

27 http://www.tts.org/images/stories/pdfs/StatementMembs-Chinese TXProg.pdf

28 http://www.ohchr.org/Documents/Issues/Business/A-HRC-17-31_ AEV.pdf

29 http://www.evb.ch/cm_data/Speech_Roche_en_1.pdf

30 http://www.roche.com/annual_general_meeting_2008_en.pdf http://www.roche.com/annual_general_meeting_2010_en.pdf

31 http://www.amnesty.ch/de/themen/wirtschaft-menschenrechte/ dok/2010/amnesty-international-calls-for-the-end-to-the-use-of- organs-from-executed-prisoners

32 https://www.dafoh.org/Statement_Clinical_Trial.php

33 Frédéric Koller, "Appel à clarifier les prélèvements d'organes sur des prisonniers en Chine," Le Temps, 4 Aug 2010. http://m.letemps.ch/Page/Uuid/72759116-a71a-11df- aeb8-0c7af7c72949/Appel_%C3%A0_clarifier_les_ pr%C3%A9l%C3%A8vements_dorganes_sur_des_prisonniers_en_ Chine

34 David Matas, "Ending Abuse of Organ Transplantation in China," The Transplantation Society Congress Vancouver, 17 Aug 2010. http://www.david-kilgour.com/2010/Aug_19_2010_01.php

35 Triodos Bank, "Pharmaceutical giant removed from investment universe," 23 Sep 2010. http://www.triodos.com/en/about-triodos-bank/news/newsletters/ newsletter-sustainability-research/pharmaceutical-company/

36 http://www.asnbank.nl/index.asp?nid=9415#525

37 http://www.roche.com/annual_general_meeting_2011_en.pdf

38 cf. footnote 18

39 https://www.dafoh.org/Forum_in_Philadelphia.php

40 http://www.gpo.gov/fdsys/pkg/CREC-2011-12-08/pdf/CREC- 2011-12-08-pt1-PgH8299-3.pdf

41 http://www.swisstransplant.org/l1/organspende-organ- transplantation-zuteilung-koordination-warteliste-gesetz-verordnungen- downloads.php?dl=1&datei=Transplantationsgesetz.pdf

42 Andrew Malone, "China's hi-tech 'death van' where criminals are executed and then their organs are sold on black market," *Mail Online*, 27 Mar 2009.
http://www.dailymail.co.uk/news/article-1165416/Chinas-hi-tech-death-van-criminals-executed-organs-sold-black-market.html

43 Max Planck, Gesellschaft "Biowissenschaftliche Forschung an Kaiser-Wilhelm-Instituten und die Verbrechen des NS-Regimes," Pressemitteilung, 12 Oct 2000. (translated from German)
http://www.mpiwg-berlin.mpg.de/KWG/Presse121000.htm

*All Internet sources were accessed last on May 2, 2012*

# The Mission of Medicine

MARIA A. FIATARONE SINGH, MD, FRACP

*The mission of medicine is the assertion and the assurance*
*of the human potential.*

– Walter Bortz, MD

       I decided to become a doctor when my beloved grandmother, Jeanne Saint-Gaudens, suffered a psychotic depression after the death of my grandfather when I was in high school. What I witnessed her endure at the hands of physicians and psychiatrists made me want to find a better way. I decided to become a geriatrician while in college, when a hip fracture and failing memory saw my grandmother again slipping between the cracks of a health care system ill-equipped to deal with frail elders, leaving her a living skeleton with pressure ulcers, dehydration, delirium, barely noticed on ward rounds, tied to the bed with restraints or too groggy from antipsychotics to look up or protest her fate. This woman who had spent her life espousing the benefits of whole foods, exercise and preventive health care, who raised me on daily episodes of Jack LaLanne and whole wheat bread long before it was fashionable, who only shopped in health food stores – this woman had been utterly failed by the medical establishment in which she had placed her faith. I knew there must be a different path. In medical school, as geriatric medicine was not yet a specialty in the USA, many of my teachers tried to dissuade me from this path, suggesting that it might be a waste to focus on this relatively uninteresting phase of the